THE UNREPENTANT CATHOLIC'S CAUTIONARY CALENDAR

The Unrepentant Catholic's Cautionary Calendar

A COMPANION VOLUME
TO THE COLLECTED WORKS

John C. Rao

AROUCA PRESS

Originally published at http://jcrao.freeshell.org.
Revised and expanded for this edition.

Copyright © John C. Rao 2022

All rights reserved:
No part of this book may be reproduced or transmitted,
in any form or by any means, without permission

ISBN: 978-1-990685-08-8 (pbk)
ISBN: 978-1-990685-09-5 (hardcover)

Arouca Press
PO Box 55003
Bridgeport PO
Waterloo, ON N2J 3G0
Canada
www.aroucapress.com
Send inquiries to info@aroucapress.com

Dedicated to Pierre Bayle (1647–1706),
Author of the First Anti-Christian Dictionary—
Because Turnabout is Fair Play

CONTENTS

Preface xi

I PREPARATION SEASON (1000S–1700S)
"Imagine all the people living for today" 1
January. 1
February. 16
March 27
April. 40

II ERUPTION SEASON (1700S–1800S)
"It's Easy if You Try". 49
May 53
June 65
July 77
August 90
September. 102

III CONSEQUENCE SEASON (1900S)
"Nothing to kill or die for" 106
October 115
November. 128

IV DENIAL SEASON (FROM ADAM & EVE TO THE PRESENT)
"Hey! I'm not the only one!" 135
December 140

V Suggestions for Monthly Outbursts
  of Spontaneous Global Joy 153

About the Author 155

PREFACE

EVEN THOUGH THEOLOGY—FOLlowed immediately by philosophy—ultimately has the most exalted role to play in explaining the Truth that sets us free, history and literature are crucially significant tools for giving men and women that clear understanding of natural human behavior that makes them see the necessity for higher wisdom and supernatural Redemption. Pastorally speaking, some of us, myself included, have primarily been confirmed in our commitment to the Catholic Faith through the aid of such tools; through our studies of mankind's yearning for God amidst its long and tragic story of sin and failure; through our awe over the magnificence of the corrective and exalting work of the transformation in Christ of natural man and society accomplished by His Mystical Body since the Incarnation of Our Lord and Savior, which took place only when "the fullness of time" had been reached, in the days of the reign of Caesar Augustus.

To paraphrase Charles Maurras, the Catholic must recognize that "all things natural belong to us." Nevertheless, our glorious Faith teaches us that the daily struggle for transformation of all things natural in Christ is one that can, indeed, be thwarted, and that this battle will continue until the Second Coming and the Final Judgment. Our Reason, once again, confirmed by our historical and literary studies, has shown us that that the Christian enterprise has been contested from the very outset, by what I like to call a "Grand Coalition of the Status Quo." This alliance involves all those individuals and social forces dedicated to "business as usual" and an acceptance of fallen, sinful nature not just as the observable normal mode of human action for most people, but also as their sole possible and highest conceivable guide. Rather than working to raise every aspect of life to serve the greater glory of God, this evil gang labors to ensure that Revelation and Grace be disdained and that redeemed mankind retreat to wallowing in degradation and despair, like a dog returning to its vomit (2 Peter 2:22).

The following volumes include a great number of my historical writings and meditations upon the struggle of the Grand Coalition of the Status Quo against the salvific activity of the Mystical Body of Christ. Although some of these pieces emphasize the victories won by the Catholic Church in a long-term war, the reality is that the "modern world" that we inhabit is one that has seen a progressive advance of the armies of the enemy. Most of the articles, in consequence, reflect the ravages of that doleful march through an ever more prostrate Christendom.

Sad as this historical development has been, we know that the victory will still be ours. Hence, even an introduction to the development of our dreary, one-dimensional Global Motherland since its remote origins in the 1000s A. D. should not be a gloomy, fatalistic enterprise. Conscious of the fact that Christ will be King of His Universe no matter what happens from moment to moment, we must always be ready to "laugh through our tears." Hence, my conviction that the tragic "meat" of this evolution should be preceded by *The Unrepentant Catholic's Cautionary Calendar,* which, in a whimsical, satirical form, uncovers the GCSQ's historical *modus operandi*—one that illustrates the typical diabolical effort to imitate God's labor in a distorted and inevitably doomed fashion, assuring the exact opposite of what it falsely claims to achieve—and the true Catholic alternative that will triumph in the end.

PREFACE   xiii

　　For this purpose, the *Cautionary Calendar* is divided into four seasons (Preparation Season, Eruption Season, Consequence Season, and Denial Season) and Twenty Six Sets of Parallel Weeks, each representing contrasting anti-Catholic and pro-Catholic themes. These follow the chronological development of modernity and its sickness-unto-death through an entire millennium. A commemoration captures the sense of each week and moves the dismal story forward. Each day is equipped with meditations designed to deconstruct the web of contradictions that shapes the Constitution of our universal Slag Heap. A day-to-day reminder of personalities and events connected both with the assault upon and the defense of the Catholic worldview is also provided. *Nota bene*: It is only fair to indicate that I encountered some surprising discrepancies with respect to a few of these dates—even regarding the birth and death of specific individuals. I sometimes had to make a choice among them that may be contested. In any case, the commemorations and the meditations count most for the historical "action." A final set of twelve monthly "outbursts of spontaneously global joy" summarizes the total fraud of an essentially irrational and totalitarian "modernity."

　　With this *Cautionary Calendar* in hand, rummage through the articles that follow, expanding upon its skeletal guide. These pieces, also arranged chronologically, sometimes overlap, and definitely indicate my own development in understanding of the issues in question and what it is that we must do to survive and rebuild a life in Christ. Catholic soldiers in the army contesting the Grand Coalition of the Status Quo unite!! You have nothing to lose but enslavement to a packet of self-destructive lies! Viva Cristo Rey!

I. PREPARATION SEASON
"Imagine all the people living for today"
(1000S–1700S)

January

1 LIFE IS HELL WEEK

Wherein we commemorate the beginning of Modernity's construction of happiness upon the belief that everything in the universe is fetid and vile. (1000s onwards) This week's commemoration is accompanied by unique suggestions for ushering in a dreadful New Year!

1/1 ALL GRIST TO MANI'S MILL DAY

Mani (217–277), the founder of Manicheanism, a Gnostic sect, sought to "deconstruct" and reinterpret every religion, its sacred books, and its customs according to his own belief that creation was evil.

¶ Canossa (1077): Emperor Henry IV (1056–1106) asks forgiveness from St. Gregory VII (1073–1085)

¶ The *Encyclopedia* project begins (1751)

¶ "Wall of Separation" (Jefferson's letter to Danbury Connecticut Baptist Association, 1802)

¶ Louis Blanqui, French radical socialist thinker, dies (1881)

¶ German Communist Party founded (1919)

¶ Fidel Castro takes power in Cuba (1959)

Wake up much too early from your New Year's Eve hangover, curse all of existence, take a copy of the *Gulag Archipelago* down from your bookshelf, deconstruct it, and admit the fact that it really treats of the gender roles of the alien forces that have cloned human beings on the earth on the model of their own riff-raff in a galaxy billions of light years away.

1/2 ROLL OUT THE BULGARS DAY

Some Gnostics, deported from Asia Minor to the area of present-day Bulgaria, began in the 1000s to go on missionary journeys to the West, especially to Italy and to southern France, to found or reform Manichean churches. Other Gnostics traveled to Bulgaria for better instruction in the evils of the universe.

¶ Fall of Granada to Ferdinand and Isabella (1492)

¶ American anarcho-syndicalist union, Industrial Workers of the World, formed (1905)

Perhaps your neighbors were deluded into thinking that they enjoyed their Christmas holidays; that they have had so much fun! Go and wake them up as well! Bring *The Gulag* with you. They also may have mistakenly thought that it dealt with the Soviet Union and labor camps. Lift up their hearts to the Truth!

1/3 DUAL TO THE DEATH DAY

Manicheans were "dualists," believing in the existence of a good, Hidden God and an evil Creation. Some thought that the Creator of evil was built into the very nature of things; some that he represented a kind of emanation from the good God gone bad. The evil universe, in general, and our evil flesh in particular, keep us separate from the good, spiritual and hidden God. The serpent in the Book of Genesis is a positive force opening our eyes to the wickedness of the Garden of Eden.

I. PREPARATION SEASON: JANUARY

❡ Martin Luther excommunicated by Pope Leo X (1521)
❡ Birth of Msgr. Félix Dupanloup, Bishop of Orléans and Liberal Catholic (1802)
❡ Resignation of Jean Villèle, one of the Legitimist Ultra leaders and chief Minister of Charles X (1828)

Your neighbors react with ill will and bad behavior to your early morning disturbance. Explain to them, as they toss you out the door, that both your misery and their uncouth behavior is perfectly understandable in this worst of all possible worlds.

1/4 WE'RE PERFECTI, YOU'RE DEFECTI DAY

A small group of "Perfect Ones," who fled the nightmare of an inherently evil world, formed the elite (and only truly complete members) of Manichean churches. The rest of men, the "Hearers," hopelessly stuck in the mud of life, might, however, dream that the *perfecti* could do something to pull them out of the muck and raise them to the Hidden God as well.

❡ Battle of Rivoli, helping to assure Napoleon's victory in Italy (1797)
❡ Death of T.S. Eliot (1965)

Compare yourself with the neighborhood wretches. You are different. You are Everysplendor! Return to the streets to spread the Good News!

1/5 ENDURA DAY

The most perfect of all Manicheans underwent the ceremony called the *endura*, and starved themselves to death.

❡ Council of Ferrara, which affirms Papal power and attempts to reconcile the Eastern Churches with Rome, opens (1438)
❡ Spartacist (Communist) Revolt in Berlin (5–15, 1919)

You have always wanted to show your mettle. Go to it!

The holidays are over and you are sick of food anyway. Start with a total renunciation of eggnog. You might even give up water, so long as you keep the scotch sours flowing. Have the neighbors pour them, though: just to maintain the purity of your hands.

1/6 WHY CAN'T A WOMAN BE LIKE A MAN DAY

An evil world really has no right to grow. Hence, the Manicheans loved contraception and hated both childbirth and the women responsible for it. Some would avert their faces and spit when they saw a newborn child appear before them.

¶ Birth of Melchior von Diepenbrock (1798–1854), Prince-Bishop of Breslau, and firm opponent of secularism

¶ Birth of Georg Phillips (1804–1872), one of the founders of the *Historisch politische Blätter*, a major journal of the 19th century German Catholic revival, and Ultramontanist canon lawyer

¶ *Longinqua oceani*, first encyclical dealing with Americanism (1895)

¶ *Mortalium animos*, encyclical dealing unfavorably with Ecumenism (1928)

If you are a woman, change into men's clothing, go to a street corner, spit and curse at everyone you see. If you are a man, change into women's clothing, then back into men's clothing, go to a street corner, spit and curse at everyone you see. The permutations on this theme are endless.

1/7 WATCH THOSE FREE SPARKS FLY DAY

Our spirits were said to be little sparks of good trapped in flesh. Free those sparks by making them aware of their complete difference from the wicked body, and they will soar to undreamed of heights.

I. PREPARATION SEASON: JANUARY

❡ Death of Catherine of Aragon (1485–1536), first wife of Henry VIII

❡ Birth of François Poulenc, composer of *Dialogue des Carmélites* (1899)

Neither aristocratic, nor bourgeois, nor proletariat morality holds you any longer. Your spirit floats above it all. The devil makes your body do anything that seems wrong to other people. Seize the moment! Let your spirit fly and your wicked body shove a copy of *The Gulag* down your neighbor's throat.

SONG OF THIS MOST BLESSED WEEK
HAPPY NEW YEAR

Happy New Year, Happy New Year.
People dying everywhere,
Hate and fear fill the air.
Happy New Year, Happy New Year.

Thus Endeth HELL WEEK ■

2 ROMANTIC LOVE WEEK

Wherein is commemorated Catholicism's insistence upon God's love for the world — thereby demonstrating to Modernity Christianity's notorious hatred of mankind. (1000s onwards)

1/8 MINE, NOT THINE DAY

Church Fathers, such as St. Irenaeus of Lyons (130?–202?), fought to prevent Gnostics from twisting the Bible to serve their own purposes. His works are an early, major source for understanding the whole nature of the orthodox conflict with Gnosticism.

❡ *Graves de communi*, encyclical dealing critically with Christian Democracy (1901)

❡ Czech National Church set up to contest papal authority (1920)

1/9 INNER MISSION DAY

Pope Innocent III (1198–1216) believed that the Church inside Europe needed a crusading, missionary work of Christian correction as much, if not more, than it was needed elsewhere; that she was, in fact, unworthy in her present condition to carry out any external crusade successfully. The Dominicans were crucial to carrying out this "inner mission" with respect to the Gnostic Catharists and their refusal to accept even the mere possibility of the correction of evil behavior.

¶ Birth of Scipione de'Ricci (1741–1810), Bishop of Pistoia, who held a Regalist and Jansenist-minded Synod in his city (1786), condemned by the Papacy in 1794

¶ Birth of Simone de Beauvoir (1908)

1/10 IT'S NOT HIS FAULT DAY

The anti-Manichean crusaders wanted to make it clear that God is not responsible for the evils of the universe; bad use of human will is the culprit.

¶ Death of Ignaz von Döllinger, German Catholic historian and opponent of the First Vatican Council (1890)

¶ *Sapientiae christianae*, on Christian responsibilities as citizens (1890)

1/11 PRIDE AND PREJUDICE DAY

Everyone is saved by recourse to the same graces; thinking otherwise is dangerous arrogance. There are no divisions between *Perfecti* and Hearers.

¶ Concordat with Spain, weakening papal power enormously (1753)

¶ Birth of Otto F. von Gierke (1841), political and legal defender of subsidiarity

1/12 ONE GOOD LEADS TO ANOTHER DAY

Building upon Scripture, Plato and ordinary experience, medieval thinkers such as St. Bernard of Clairvaux (1090–1154), demonstrated the "hierarchy of values" leading from good earthly things to even better supernatural perfections.

¶ Banishment of Joseph Fouché, regicide and founder of Napoleon's police force (1816)

¶ Birth of Cardinal Louis Billot (1846)

1/13 CRÈCHE DAY

Assisi was a Manichean center. St. Francis developed the use of the crèche at the Christmas season as a means of fighting Gnostic flesh and child hatred, and demonstrating to the population what was truly at stake in this conflict.

¶ Roman population's attack vs. Bassville and La Flotte, French revolutionary representatives in the Eternal City (1793)

¶ Death of Joseph Kleutgen, Neo-Thomist and *peritus* at the First Vatican Council (1883)

1/14 WHAT ELSE DID YOU EXPECT? DAY

A dignified use of the human body is inextricably tied together with a sense of the goodness of God's creation, the reality of human freedom, and the need to use that freedom to follow the Divine Plan rather than to reject it. Thus it was no surprise that some Gnostics believed that once the spiritual "sparks" inside them had learned about their distinction from their evil bodies, they could then consider themselves to be liberated, allowing their flesh to sink into the mud of vice to which it belonged. An example of this type of Manichean approach were the "Free Spirit" heretics active in varied places by the 1200s/1300s.

- ⁋ Murder of the Papal Legate in Toulouse (1208)
- ⁋ Death of Paolo Sarpi, anti-papal Venetian priest (1623)
- ⁋ Revolt of the *lazzari* in Naples versus the French (1799)
- ⁋ Orsini's bomb against Napoleon III (1858)

Thus Endeth ROMANTIC LOVE WEEK ∎

3 THERE OUGHT TO BE A LAW WEEK

Wherein is commemorated Modernity's pursuit of its love of order and justice through slavish, uncritical adulation of ancient thought and jurisprudence. (1000s onwards)

1/15 IF THIS IS CLASSICAL IT MUST BE GOOD DAY

Some medieval thinkers were so aware of the glories of ancient Greece and Rome that they were ready to treat anything coming from these sources as obviously good. This had a great impact once the full body of texts on Roman Law started to become available in the 1000s, and when Aristotle's works were translated into Latin in the 1100s and 1200s.

- ⁋ Theophilanthropy (1797)
- ⁋ Birth of Pierre Proudhon, early and extremely interesting French anarchist (1809)
- ⁋ Death of Rosa Luxembourg and Wilhelm Liebknecht, Spartacist leaders (1919)

1/16 ANGRY BUREAUCRAT DAY

Civil servants from ancient Rome and Constantinople were often upset by the intrusion of Christian ideals and institutional influence in the life of the God-State. Growing medieval civil services began to feel the same irritation as they gained deeper understanding of the fullness of Roman Law from the 1000s onwards.

I. PREPARATION SEASON: JANUARY 9

❡ Death of Edward Gibbon (1794)
❡ Proclamation of the Reconciliation of Jews and Christians in *The Globe*, the Saint-Simonian newspaper (1832)
❡ Birth of Heinrich Denifle, Ultramontanist historian-theologian (1844)

1/17 PETULANT AMBITIOUS STUDENT DAY

Students gathering in centers such as Bologna, where Law was especially studied, left University looking for positions. Some posts were available with the newly growing bureaucracies. Legal graduates eager for honors could help to provide learned justifications for the anger and lust of bureaucrats.

❡ Gregory XI returns to Rome (1377)
❡ Birth of Pius V (1504)
❡ Marriage as Civil Contract in Austria (1783)
❡ Treaty of Montluçon (1800)
❡ Birth of Léon Harmel (1829), Catholic Social activist
❡ Rudolf Virchow's call for *Kulturkampf* (1873)

1/18 LITTLE CAESAR DAY

France became an early center for student-bureaucrat alliances. French kings, from the early 1200s onwards, were told that they could and should act in their own realms as the most pompous of Roman Emperors had done.

❡ Pius II, *Execrabilis* (1460)
❡ Birth of Fr. Agostino Gemelli, OFM (1878), founder of the *Cattolica* in Milan
❡ Birth of Cardinal Alfredo Schuster (1880)
❡ Appeal of the Italian *Partito Popolare* to all free and strong men (1919)

1/19 FAR-FETCHED FLIMSY EXCUSE DAY

Philip the Fair (1285–1314) of France began to take serious action against the prerogatives of the Church and other institutions in French life in order to build up the power of a model Roman State. Cases were developed on the basis of distorted documents, propaganda, and the calling of stage-managed assemblies to show the existence of popular support for his crimes.

¶ Chancellor Maupeou vs. French *parlements* (1771)
¶ Birth of Auguste Comte (1798)

1/20 PROCEDURAL HOO-HA DAY

Philip the Fair and his legal advisors were none too squeamish regarding those procedures to be followed, twisted or ignored entirely. This was clear in their actions versus Boniface VIII (1294–1303) and the Templars (1307), both of whom they accused of devil worship.

¶ Vision of Marie Alphonse Ratisbonne (1842)
¶ The American Civil Liberties Union is founded (1920)

1/21 IMPERIALIST CONTRADICTION DAY

The Holy Roman Empire became deeply involved in the legalist-student-heresy game in the early 1300s, when William of Ockham (c. 1285–1349) and Marsilius of Padua (1290–1343) joined hands in support of Louis IV (1314–1347). Arguments in support of absolute imperial power also emphasized the importance of basing such absolute power upon a democratic base of support—but one that was sufficiently manipulated as to yield the desired "spontaneous," "popular" results before the People knew that they desired to express them.

¶ First Anabaptist baptisms at Zollikon (1525)
¶ Procession vs. the Protestant Placards in Paris (1535)
¶ Birth of Archbishop Clemens Droste-zu-Vischering of Cologne (1773)

I. PREPARATION SEASON: JANUARY 11

❡ Execution of Louis XVI (1793)
❡ Martyrs of Laval (1794)

Thus Endeth THERE OUGHT TO BE A LAW WEEK ■

4 THE LAW CAN BE AN ASS WEEK

Wherein is commemorated that Catholic subservience to authority which is shown through merciless personal soul-searching, self-sacrifice and violent death. (1000s onwards)

1/22 BEAT HIM TILL HE CONFESSES HIS INNOCENCE DAY

Tertullian already demonstrated in the 190s and early 200s the contradictions of the Roman State's approach towards the Christians. For example, one normally used "persuasion" in order to get a confession of guilt from suspected criminals. Christians, on the other hand, were tortured until they confessed that they were innocent of the charge of embracing Christianity, so that the government could let these people—whom it knew to be law-abiding in every other respect—go free.

❡ *Testem benevolentiae*, Apostolic letter to Cardinal Gibbons (1899)
❡ Roe vs. Wade (1972)

1/23 SAILING TO BYZANTIUM DAY

Roman pontiffs in the 500s and 600s had to answer to the Emperors in Constantinople for their actions. These would kidnap, torture and send them into exile to starve to death if they "disrupted the legal order"—even when that legal order had no business dictating its teachings to the Church. Pope St. Martin I (649–655) and his Greek adviser St. Maximus Confessor (580–662) were, perhaps, the most famous victims of this procedure.

¶ *Gloriosam ecclesiam* (1318, vs. the Fraticelli)
¶ Birth of Stendhal (1783)
¶ Parthenopean Republic (1799)
¶ Birth of Antonio Gramsci (1891)

1/24 RECUPERATION DAY

Many Christians thought that apostolic tradition required treating the Emperor as the highest authority in the Church as well as in the State. Gregory VII (1073–1085) showed that this was a false "custom," ennobled by years of abuse, and very much tied with an unacceptable adulation of the Emperor Constantine. The Church, to be truly apostolic, needed freedom over her own internal life.

¶ Emperor Ferdinand II declares Wallenstein a traitor (1634)
¶ Vera Zasulich's assault on Fyodor Trepov (1878)
¶ Foundation of the World Economic Forum by Klaus Schwab (1971)

1/25 DON'T PLAY WITH MATCHES DAY

Some canon lawyers were so enamored of Roman Law as a universal model as to presume that the Church herself could be treated as a kind of legal business. St. Bernard warned against this mentality to his protégé, Pope Eugenius III (1145–1151), insisting that it would lead to a bureaucratization of the Roman Church.

¶ Holy Synod (1721)
¶ Birth of Joseph Görres (1776), German Catholic leader
¶ Destruction of the German Ecclesiastical States (1803)
¶ Concordat of Fontainebleau (1813)
¶ Antwerp Declaration of the Comte de Chambord (1872)
¶ John XXIII tells a group of Cardinals of his plan to call a Council (1959)
¶ *Consilium* (1965)

I. PREPARATION SEASON: JANUARY

1/26 MAKE MY DAY DAY

Boniface VIII, himself a lawyer, faced down the absolutist, legalist designs of Philip the Fair. He courageously offered "even my neck" to the bullies sent by the French King to work him over in his castle at Anagni in 1302.

⁋ Pius IV Confirms Trent (1564)

⁋ Death of Gambetta (1882)

1/27 YOU CANNOT BE IN TWO PLACES AT ONCE DAY

Alas, the legalist mentality was accompanied by the development of an ever more bureaucratized Roman Church. It offered arguments justifying the appointment of Roman bureaucrats to bishoprics and abbatial positions to obtain revenues that could be used to pay them. Such appointments generally ensured that dioceses would never see their bishops, who stayed at their curial posts in Rome. Absenteeism was especially guaranteed when one man would be given the title of Ordinary in more than one place at the same time.

⁋ Charles Perrault's poem, *The Age of Louis the Great*, read at the French Academy (1687)

⁋ Birth of Mozart (1756)

1/28 AGGRAVATED AVIGNONITIS DAY

After the Papacy moved to Avignon in 1312, it succumbed to ever greater bureaucratization, bureaucratic legalization, and open money grubbing. Avignon became a by-word for corruption.

⁋ Death of Charlemagne (814)

⁋ Emperor Charles V opens the Diet of Worms (1521)

Thus Endeth THE LAW CAN BE AN ASS WEEK ∎

5 MERELY WORDS WEEK

Wherein is commemorated Modernity's beginning eagerness to relearn the ancient Sophist lesson that it does not matter what you say but how you say it. (1300s onwards)

1/29 IF IT MAKES SENSE, IT MUST BE MEANINGLESS DAY

Extreme Nominalists, like William of Ockham, were convinced that any philosophical attempt to go beyond the appreciation of pure "data," and any effort to make meaningful statements about important concepts such as "justice," were absolutely hopeless. The result could be nothing more than the production of hot air.

¶ Birth of Thomas Paine (1737)
¶ Death of Henri de la Rochejaquelein (1794)

1/30 IT COULD HAVE BEEN THE OPPOSITE DAY

Nominalists believed that God's omnipotence involved God's unlimited will to do what He wished. He made a world in which good deeds were rewarded and bad ones punished. But He was so powerful he could have done the opposite if he had wanted to do so.

¶ Charles I executed (1649)
¶ Excommunication of the Duke of Parma (1768)
¶ Resignation of Marshal MacMahon (1879)

1/31 UNEXAMINED FAITH DAY

Nominalists said that Faith alone could give solid information about truth, goodness and beauty. But Faith could not in any way be explored and understood through the use of philosophy—which, they explained, cannot tell us anything meaningful whatsoever.

I. PREPARATION SEASON: JANUARY

- ¶ Helvetius' *De l'Esprit* condemned (1759)
- ¶ Birth of Ludwig von Pastor (1854)
- ¶ Death of Franz Josef von Buss (1878)
- ¶ Exile of Trotsky (1929)

February

2/1 LET'S HANG ON TO WHAT WE'VE NOT DAY

The 1300s were a pretty awful period generally. Medieval men like Petrarch (1304–1374), who admired the ancients, felt that one way out of the current mess would be by means of exploring what these same ancients would have done to deal with modern problems. One needed to turn back to the roots, but most especially to those that had been neglected, like literary, historical and generally more "human" roots, as opposed to logical and mathematical themes, which had already been explored *ad nauseam*.

¶ Murder of Carlos I, King of Portugal, and his heir (1908)

¶ Death of Venerable Ramón Ibarra y Gonzalez, Archbishop of Puebla (1917)

2/2 SECOND CHILDHOOD DAY

Going back to one's roots is fine—so long as he does not think that nothing has happened in the interim to alter his life, perhaps even irrevocably. A revived childhood is not an original childhood, but a second childhood, and often ridiculous in consequence.

¶ Crowning of Otto as Roman Emperor (962)

¶ French Occupation of Rome (1808)

¶ Election of Gregory XVI (1831)

¶ Crusade of Prayer (1930)

¶ Congress begins work of ending Prohibition (1933)

I. PREPARATION SEASON: FEBRUARY 17

2/3 UNINVITED GUEST DAY

Admirers of both Greek and Roman literature as well as Platonic Philosophy might have expected only good to come from their efforts to revive knowledge of such disciplines. But the ancients had many temptations—ranging from skepticism to cynicism to magic and to gross immorality. Bring ancient life back uncritically and you might get more than you bargained for!

¶ Johannes Gutenberg dies (1468)
¶ General Monck's army reaches London (1660)

2/4 NEVER CROSS A HUMANIST DAY

Humanists proved to be eager for positions to support their work. They could be vicious if not rewarded. When they turned vicious, all of their newly nurtured facility with Latin, Greek and Hebrew was aimed, with bitter satire, at reviling those who had thwarted them. The historical record has been badly distorted in consequence.

¶ Revolution in Papal States (1831)
¶ Cardinal Louis de Bonald condemns the Gallican manual of Dupin (1845)
¶ Yalta (4–11, 1945)

Thus Endeth MERELY WORDS WEEK ■

6 MORE THAN WORDS CAN TELL WEEK

Wherein is commemorated Catholicism's thick-headed stupidity—as displayed by its avoiding temptations to abandon either Truth or Beauty. (1000s–1500s)

2/5 BALANCED DIET DAY

Christians were already learning from the time of Clement of Alexandria (100s), Origen (200s), and St. Gregory of Nyssa (300s) of the need to combine Tradition and

Scripture on the one hand with the Classical Tradition on the other. The early medieval educational focus on the alliance of Christianity with the "Seven Liberal Arts" reflected this concern.

¶ Françoise Mézière guillotined (1794)
¶ Birth of Johannes von Geissel, Cardinal Archbishop of Cologne (1796)
¶ Birth of Olympe-Philippe Gerbet, Bishop of Perpignan (1798)
¶ Birth of J.K. Huysmans (1848)
¶ *Quod nunquam* vs. Prussia (1875)
¶ Mexican Constitution (1917)

2/6 TRANSLATION DAY

Educated ancients knew both Greek and Latin, and therefore did not need translations. Such a need did develop by the 400s, but could not satisfactorily be addressed at that time. Instead, translation of Greek works into Latin, sometimes directly, sometimes through Arabic, was only extensively undertaken in the 1100s and 1200s, primarily in Spain and Sicily.

¶ Charles of Anjou defeats Manfred (1266)
¶ Grand Duke flees Tuscany (1849)
¶ Guevara y Lera becomes archbishop of Caracas (1853)
¶ Birth of Amintore Fanfani (1908)
¶ Paris anti-Republican Riots (1934)

2/7 HIT THE BOOKS DAY

The High Middle Ages saw the possibility of developing more profound learning in the institutions that came to be called universities. Built on the models of the Universities of Bologna or Paris, such centers became the pride of Popes, Emperors and Kings, all of whom encouraged study within their precincts.

I. PREPARATION SEASON: FEBRUARY

❡ Attack on Jesuits in Parma (7–8, 1768)
❡ Belgian Constitution (1831)
❡ Death of Pius IX (1878)

2/8 WATCH YOUR REDUCTIONIST STEP DAY

There was much literary focus in schools that never became universities, like the one at Chartres. Universities proper, however, tended to become focused mostly on legal or Aristotelian philosophical studies. Men like John of Salisbury were frightened by this trend, and warned of its one-sided consequences.

❡ Death of Mary, Queen of Scots (1587)
❡ *Nobilissima gallorum gens*, Leo XIII on the religious question in France (1884)

2/9 THERE'S ALWAYS ROOM FOR MORE DAY

One branch of learning that was still missing in the 1300s was that of Greek studies, including the study of Plato. A new knowledge of Greek and Plato added to the store of western scholarship by the 1400s, although this, too, could be—and often was—turned into a one-sided obsession.

❡ Proclamation of Roman Republic (1849)
❡ Death of Johann Baptist Heinrich, editor of *Der Katholik* of Mainz (1891)

2/10 HERE'S HOW YOU DO IT DAY

Despite the reductionism of so many Humanists and philosophers, the 1400s also saw the work of great Christian Humanists, who were still able to combine theology, philosophy and literary studies in a harmonious way. Some of these men, like Nicholas V, became popes as well.

❡ Last Mass in Basel (1529)
❡ Treaty of Paris (1763)

⁋ Revolutionary French General Berthier arrives in Rome (1798)

⁋ Pius IX's "Blessing on Italy" (1848)

⁋ *Arcanum divinae* (1880)

⁋ Death of Cardinal Aloysius Stepinac, Archbishop of Zagreb (1960)

2/11 LIFT UP YOUR HEADS DAY

Mysticism flourished in the 1300s and 1400s, partly due to the desire present in every age to raise the spirit above purely earthly things — but especially at this time, as a reaction to the previous era's exaggerated emphasis on the sole glories of logical thinking.

⁋ Lourdes apparition (1858)

⁋ *Vehementer nos* (1906)

⁋ Lateran accords (1929)

Thus Endeth MORE THAN WORDS CAN TELL WEEK ∎

7 APOCALYPSE NOW WEEK

Wherein is commemorated Modernity's temptation to build hope for the future upon an abandonment of existing reality. (1000s–1500s)

2/12 WE'RE ON THE ROAD TO ATLANTIS DAY

The calling of the First Crusade (1095) unwittingly encouraged certain popular apocalyptic notions. Mobs, often thinking that they were headed towards the Heavenly Jerusalem as opposed to the merely earthly one presently occupied by the Turks, stampeded through the Rhine Valley, purifying the world while passing through. Clergy, as well as Jews, were among their favorite targets.

⁋ Birth of Charles Darwin (1809)

⁋ First papal radio broadcast (1931)

I. PREPARATION SEASON: FEBRUARY

2/13 IT'S JUST AROUND THE CORNER DAY

The apocalyptic spirit reached a fever pitch by the 1100s and 1200s. One exegete whose work became important in stimulating this was Joachim of Fiore (1132–1202), who spoke of the "three ages of the world" and the imminent coming of the reign of the Holy Spirit.

¶ Birth of Talleyrand (1754)
¶ Suppression of Perpetual Vows in France (1790)
¶ Massacre of Catholics at Uzès (1791)

2/14 DIRTY RATS IN THE WAY DAY

The coming of the Holy Spirit required purification of the corruption of this world, by means of the work of angelic priests and popes. Boniface VIII was despised by many apocalyptic believers as an agent of corruption responsible for removing one such holy but politically naive "Angelic Pope"—Celestine V (1294).

¶ Death of the Duke de Berry (1820)
¶ Sack of St. Germain l'Auxerrois (1831)

2/15 DIVESTMENT DAY

Preparation for the reign of the Holy Spirit also called for an end to property. The Spiritual Franciscans, who took St. Francis' call to poverty literally, balked at efforts to restrict the rigor of his appeal. Some became apocalyptic in consequence of the success of the "laxists," turning poverty into the highest of virtues, even more important than that of charity.

¶ Birth of Galileo (1564)
¶ The Peace of La Jaunaie in the Vendèe (1795)
¶ Roman Republic (1798)
¶ Sack of Archbishopric of Paris—some sources say the 13th (1831)

2/16 THE PROOF IS IN THE BUBOS DAY

The Black Death began its first of many visits to Europe in 1348. The suffering and devastation that it brought in its train convinced many, like the wandering Flagellants, that the end must truly be near.

- ¶ Birth of Henry Adams (1838)
- ¶ Spanish Republic (1873)
- ¶ *Au milieu des sollicitudes* (1892)
- ¶ Popular Front victory in Spain (1936)

2/17 NEW WORLD SYMPHONY DAY

Apocalyptic thinking in no way led everyone to despair. Many thought that the "end times" would usher in a thousand years of paradisical conditions. The idea of a "New World" as a place for a "fresh start", free from the corruptions of the past, wherein such blissful conditions could flourish, appealed to a vast audience.

- ¶ Giordano Bruno burned (1600)
- ¶ Birth of Edgar Quinet (1803)
- ¶ *Ausgleich* and Creation of Austria-Hungary (1867)

2/18 YOU CAN'T MAKE AN OMELETTE WITHOUT BREAKING EGGS DAY

Still, the idea of a purification period before the new age might be inaugurated, seemed to be appropriate to many. The years preceding and accompanying the start of the Reformation were rich in attempted purifications, such as in the work of Thomas Müntzer (1489–1525) and the Anabaptists at Münster (1534–1535).

- ¶ Death of Martin Luther (1546)
- ¶ Consecration of Ramón Méndez in Caracas (1828)
- ¶ Trial of Dom Vital in Brazil (1874)

Thus Endeth APOCALYPSE NOW WEEK ■

8 DON'T HOLD YOUR BREATH WEEK

Wherein is commemorated Catholicism's dampening of apocalyptic fun by reminding people of continued daily chores. (1000s–1500s)

2/19 GET A MAP DAY

The Church, since the time of their first appearance with the Montanists of the 200s, has never encouraged apocalyptic marches on Heavenly Jerusalems. This is one of the reasons why she has regularly been the target of abuse of mad seers and false prophets.

¶ Death of Mother Agnes Arnauld (1672)
¶ Treaty of Tolentino (1797)

2/20 WHAT YOU SEE IS WHAT YOU GET DAY

The Church, following the arguments of the Fathers, has taught that the conditions under which we live will last until the end, and not be purified by any reign of the Holy Spirit. The Kingdom of God is to be established now, but under present conditions, working with the realities of an unchangingly sinful mankind.

¶ Death of Emperor Joseph II (1790)
¶ Pope Pius VI forced to leave Rome (1798)
¶ Execution of Andreas Hofer (1810)
¶ Birth of Georges Bernanos (1888)

2/21 THE BUMS YOU WILL ALWAYS HAVE WITH YOU DAY

From the time of the Donatists, fought so ably by St. Augustine, the Church has made it clear that good and bad are inexorably mixed together, even in the highest ranks of the hierarchy. No sorting out will occur before Judgment Day.

¶ Birth of John Henry Newman (1801)

¶ Birth of Heinrich Rommen (1897), Catholic political thinker

¶ Death of Cardinal Eugène Tisserant (1972), a man of some ecumenical mystery

2/22 PREFERENTIAL OPTION FOR EVERYBODY DAY

The voluntary embrace of poverty can be a very good thing indeed. Still, it can become evil if it is treated as a necessity, or if those who adopt it also adopt an arrogant attitude towards anyone possessing goods. Fights over this issue reached a peak of excitement during the reign of Pope John XXII (1316–1334).

¶ *Inter cunctas* and *In eminentis* (1418)

¶ Paris Riots and Revolution (1848)

¶ Birth of Edward Kennedy (1932)

2/23 JUST ANOTHER PRECIPICE DAY

The Black Death was not necessarily a harbinger of the end. It did not even strike everywhere in Europe. Still, those looking for grounds for Penance could use it as a call to action, as they also could the eruption of the Ottoman Turks into Europe in the 1300s, their capture of Constantinople in 1453, and the horrific scandal of the Great Western Schism—which divided Christendom in allegiance to two and three popes (1378–1415).

¶ Apotheosis of the revolutionary figure, Duphat (1798)

¶ Assassination of Fr. Joseph Leo Heinrichs, OFM, by an Anarchist in Colorado (1908)

2/24 NEW WORLD ODOR DAY

Fresh beginnings still involve the activity of fallen men carting old baggage along with them to their "fresh venues." The discovery of the New World quickly brought

I. PREPARATION SEASON: FEBRUARY

in its train many evils, including the widespread rebirth of slavery.
- ¶ *Clericos laicos* (1296)
- ¶ Birth of Emperor Charles V (1500)
- ¶ Seven Articles of Schlechtheim (1527)
- ¶ Abdication of Louis-Philippe (1848)

2/25 COLD WESTPHALIAN SHOWER DAY

The reign of the pure in Münster in 1534–1535 turned almost immediately into a macabre horror show, hardly reminiscent of the work of the Holy Spirit.
- ¶ Deposition of Elizabeth I (1570)
- ¶ Dissolution of the Ecclesiastical Principalities (1803)
- ¶ Victor Hugo's *Hernani* (1830)

Thus Endeth DON'T HOLD YOUR BREATH WEEK ■

9 A THOUSAND SINS WEEK

Wherein is commemorated Protestantism's great boost to human dignity by its insistence upon just how hopelessly wretched and un-free people really are. (1500s onwards)

2/26 BACKWOODS BELLOWING AND BONFIRE DAY

Wittenberg was a provincial backwater, experiencing a building boom due to the recent creation of a university therein. It was under the control of a prince who wished to demonstrate how important his capital really could be. Much of the support for Luther (1483–1546) came from provincial rage against the centers of cosmopolitan Catholic culture.
- ¶ Death of Joseph de Maistre (1821)
- ¶ Call for Catholic Associations in Spain (1843)
- ¶ Death of Cardinal Merry del Val (1930)

2/27 NO REDEEMING VALUE DAY

Men, for Luther, were totally depraved after Original Sin. Nothing that they could do could please God. Even their so-called good deeds masqueraded a thousand sins. In fact, they were only allowed eternal life on sufferance, as a heap of dung covered by the snow of God's grace.

- Condemnation of Febronius' *De statu ecclesiae* (1764)
- Signing of order suppressing the Jesuits in Spain (for March 31–April 3, 1767)
- The Oxford Movement's Tract 90 (1841)

2/28 THEY THOUGHT THEY WERE FREE DAY

There was no possibility of free action in Luther and the other initial Reformers' theology. Men were irrevocably doomed to do evil. Ergo, in its inimitable way, modern logic finds such figures to be eminently suited to enter into its pantheon of freedom fighters.

- Birth of Ernest Renan (1823)
- Birth of Albert de Mun (1841), Catholic Social Leader
- Third Carlist War ends (1876)

March

3/1 READ IT, RIP IT APART, REWRITE IT DAY

For Reformers like Luther, who had adopted both Nominalism and Humanism, only Faith as taught through literary texts could be redemptive. The Bible became the source of all Christian Truth, though that same Bible had to be interpreted in line with their initial theory of Total Depravity. If sections of the Bible did not lend themselves to such an interpretation, one was obliged to reject them as invalid.

¶ The incident at Vassy and the beginning of the French Religious Wars (1562)

¶ *The Spectator* (1712)

¶ Birth of Cardinal François de Richard of Paris (1819)

¶ Dissolution of the Worker Priests (1954)

3/2 CHERCHEZ LA FEMME DAY

Some Reform was honestly pursued by women, such as Jeanne d'Albrette of Navarre. Some Reform was instituted because of problems with women, such as that of Henry VIII (1509–1547).

¶ Birth of Leo XIII (1810)

¶ Birth of Bishop Claude Plantier of Nîmes (1813)

¶ Birth of Fr. Herman Schaepman (1844), Dutch Catholic political leader

¶ Comintern Founded (1919)

¶ Birth of Mikhail Gorbachev (1931)

¶ Election of Pope Pius XII (1939)

3/3 TOO MANY CHEFS DAY

Protestantism rapidly divided into innumerable sects. This became an argument against its validity, exploited by Catholic apologists such as Bishop Bossuet (1627–1704) of Meaux.

¶ Fr. Charles Maignen's *L'Americanisme mystique* (1897)

¶ Fusillade of Champels and the Quarrel of the Inventories (1906)

3/4 ACT BEFORE YOU THINK DAY

Protestants were aware that their divisions were an apologetic problem. This was one of the causes for the growth of Pietism, which became, in effect, the state religion of the Kingdom of Prussia in the 1700s. Pietists avoided doctrinal discussions and focused — ironically enough, given Protestantism's founding principles — on Christian good deeds. They argued that one could be sure that God had blessed their labors if their activity proved to be successful.

¶ Emperor Frederick Barbarossa takes power (1152)

¶ First tavern in North America opens in Boston (1634)

¶ Ordination of Fr. Pierre Coudrin in revolutionary France (1792)

¶ Reestablishment of Dutch Catholic dioceses (1853)

Thus Endeth A THOUSAND SINS WEEK ■

10 SINNERS IN THE PIAZZA NAVONA WEEK

Wherein is commemorated Catholicism's supposed failure to understand the whole man and his dreams by its recognition of both the reality of his flaws and his need to rise above them. (1400s onwards)

3/5 USELESS CHATTER DAY

The Great Western Schism was indeed a disaster. Many suggestions for resolving it were bandied about, especially at the University of Paris. One solution was to resolve and rebuild the Church on the basis of the power of Councils (Conciliarism). Unfortunately, Councils such as that at Pisa (1409) worsened the Schism. Even the Council of Constance (1414–1418), which ended it, helped to strip the Church of needed resources and make it more nationally focused and secular in character.

¶ Jansenist Appeal versus *Unigenitus* (1717)
¶ Birth of Karl Rahner (1904)
¶ Death of Joseph Stalin (1953)

3/6 SELF-INDULGENCE DAY

Practically everyone seemed to be secular-minded in the 1400s. The Popes, stripped of resources, dedicated much of their time to the exploitation of the Papal States; Cardinals, bishops and priests to the accumulation of benefices and the reduction of spiritual labors; the laity, to the retention and extension of its privileges over Church affairs.

¶ Nicholas V becomes Pope (1447)
¶ Act of Restitution in the Holy Roman Empire (1629)

3/7 GASPING FOR SPIRITUAL BREATH DAY

Genuine Church reformers among popes, cardinals, bishops and religious found the hunt for restoration of a more spiritual outlook very, very trying. Still, joint clerical-lay movements like that of the Brethren of the Common Life, along with Franciscans and others eager to follow their founders' Rule more closely, did begin to make some progress. Indeed, practically all of the great forces that would labor in the Catholic Reformation were in place before the Protestants began their own dubious reform activity.

¶ Restoration of the Jesuits in Russia (1801)
¶ Excommunication of Alfred Loisy (1908)
¶ Emperor Charles attempts coup in Hungary (1921)
¶ Engelbert Dollfuss suspends Austrian Parliament (1933)
¶ Death of Leonid Feodorov, Exarch of the Russian Byzantine Catholic Church (1935)

3/8 YOU SIMPLY NEVER KNOW DAY

The Spirit blows where He wills. No one would have expected that the corrupt Farnese Pope, Paul III (1534-1549) would be the one to set the Catholic Reformation in motion with official support.

¶ Henry VIII recognized as Supreme Head of the Church in England (1531)
¶ February (March) Revolution Begins in Russia (1917)
¶ First US combat forces arrive in Vietnam (1965)

3/9 SELF-CORRECTION DAY

The Catholic Reformation involved an enormous self-purification effort. One official stimulus to this came with the report on the "crimes" of the Church commissioned by Paul III, which placed much of the blame

on the corruption of the Papacy itself. Another was, of course, the Council of Trent (1545–1563).
℣ Birth of the Count Honoré de Mirabeau (1739)
℣ Adam Smith publishes *The Wealth of Nations* (1776)

3/10 ELEGANT SUFFICIENCY DAY

The Jesuits and other Catholic reformers believed that men had to work freely with grace in order to lift up all of nature to the "greater glory of God." God had given to His People sufficient gifts to fulfill this task with style. Hence, the Catholic world burst forth in that hymn of nature to the Divine that characterized Baroque architecture and city planning.
℣ Balthasar Hubmaier burned in Vienna (1528)
℣ Birth of Friedrich Schlegel (1772)
℣ Foundation of the Revolutionary Tribunal (1793)
℣ Vendée Uprising (1793)
℣ Death of Giuseppe Mazzini (1872)
℣ Mayor Karl Lueger of Vienna dies (1910)

3/11 ALL ROADS LEAD TO ROME DAY

The Catholic Reformation made the Papacy a central force in Church reform. It also beautified Rome. But, perhaps most importantly, it coincided with a worldwide extension of Catholic missionary activity, which Rome was eager to have a guiding role in directing through such institutions as the Congregation for the Propagation of the Faith.
℣ Counterrevolution starts in the Vendée (1793)
℣ Birth of Fr. Giovanni Perrone, SJ (1794)
℣ Death of Edgar Mortara (1940)

Thus Endeth SINNERS IN THE PIAZZA NAVONA WEEK ■

11 WITH FRIENDS LIKE THIS, WHO NEEDS ENEMIES WEEK

Wherein is commemorated the modern State's efforts to defend Christianity by redefining what it is and what it can and cannot do. (1500s–1700s)

3/12 ENOUGH IS ENOUGH DAY

Religious wars abounded in the years from the 1540s until 1648, and even beyond. These generally became entangled with all sorts of political and social issues. By the time of the Treaty of Westphalia (1648), political leaders wanted Church interference in international affairs reduced to a minimum, seeing it to be something dangerous for the stability of the ruling dynasties.

¶ Election of Pope Urban II (1088)

¶ Knights of the Faith and the Coup of Bordeaux aiding the Restoration (1814)

3/13 SIMPLY DIVINE DAY

One obvious way of trying to deal with internal religious divisions was to emphasize the Divine Right of the State, embodied in the King—himself a scion of a particular Dynasty—as the final judge and guarantor of Order.

¶ Birth of Emperor Joseph II (1741)

¶ Vienna Revolution (1848)

¶ Death of Charles de Montalembert (1870)

¶ Assassination of Emperor Alexander II (1881)

3/14 IT'S NONE OF YOUR BUSINESS DAY

Divine Right kings and other rulers did not appreciate the interference of Rome in the affairs of the Church in their bailiwicks. Hence, the Bourbon Family's support

I. PREPARATION SEASON: MARCH   33

for Gallicanism, which emphasized local French rights, and other parochial phenomena.
¶ Death of Einhard, biographer of Charlemagne (840)
¶ Election of Pope Pius VII (1800)
¶ Papal *Statuto* in Rome (1848)
¶ Death of Karl Marx (1883)
¶ *Mit brennender sorge* (1937)

3/15 TIRESOME ALLIES DAY

Portugal, Spain and then France tried very hard to maintain control over the missions, often with very little interest in pursuing missionary goals. Hence, Rome and the Congregation for the Propagation of the Faith often found themselves locked in battle with their supposed protectors.
¶ Falloux Law on Catholic Education in France (1850)
¶ Resignation of Cardinal Achlle Liénhart of Lille (1968)
¶ Feast of Clemens Maria Hofbauer (1751–1820)

3/16 TOUCHY, TOUCHY DAY

States became very sensitive about offenses to their "honor." Respect for their "honor," unfortunately, often involved allowing their embassies in Rome to be used as havens for outlaws and other riffraff who could be utilized to embarrass the Papal Government.
¶ Birth of Fr. Franz Hitze (1851), Catholic social leader
¶ Birth of Count August Cardinal von Galen of Münster (1878)

3/17 SEE HOW VERY STRONG THEY ARE DAY

Certain countries untroubled by Rome, doctrinal disputes, and the interference of powerful Church forces in secular affairs became rich and powerful—especially eighteenth century Britain and Prussia. Their success, alone, seemed reason enough to justify their use as models by other lands, including supposedly Catholic ones.

❡ Foundation of the Kingdom of Italy (1861)

❡ Assassination of Jules Ferry, French Republican leader (1893)

3/18 NOT TOO SPICY DAY

Mysticism seemed to be pointless in a world that became more and more concerned for social order, prosperity and raw power alone — once again, along the lines of what could be observed in Britain and Prussia.

❡ Burning of the Templars (1314)

❡ Milanese Five Days (17–23, 1848)

❡ *Iamdudum cernimus* (1861)

❡ Paris Commune uprising (1871)

❡ Death of Fr. Pietro Tacchi-Venturi, SJ (1956)

Thus Endeth WITH FRIENDS LIKE THIS WHO NEEDS ENEMIES WEEK ■

12 INCOHERENT FUMBLING WEEK

Wherein is commemorated Catholicism's demonstration of its monolithic steam roller character by its pathetic indulgence in self-debilitating internal quarrels. (1600s–1700s)

3/19 TIRESOME DISPUTE DAY

The Council of Trent taught that Grace and Free Will were both needed to achieve Redemption, but did not go into great depth as to the exact relationship of the two. Dominicans and Jesuits argued furiously, often uncharitably, and ultimately to no avail about these issues, leading to a general frustration with doctrinal disputes.

❡ Cadiz Constitution (1812)

❡ Pius VII freed (1814)

I. PREPARATION SEASON: MARCH   35

℣ Louis XVIII flees Paris (1815)
℣ Prussian Revolution (1848)
℣ Birth of Fr. Joseph Pohle (1852)
℣ *Divini redemptoris* (1937)

3/20 WHO'S AFRAID OF THE CELESTIAL KINGDOM DAY

Another object of dispute was Jesuit missionary methods in China, bitterly contested, ultimately to the detriment of the Jesuits, by many Dominicans and Franciscans. One motive for the dispute was the extent to which cooperation with the local culture was valid. Another was the seeming support Jesuit admiration of China gave to the idea that a high civilization could be constructed on a philosophy such as Confucianism, with no knowledge of the revealed Law of God.

℣ Death of Isaac Newton (1727)
℣ Execution of the Duc d'Enghien (1804)
℣ Birth of Msgr. Frédéric de Mérode (1820)

3/21 COULD YOU PLEASE BE QUIET DAY

Miguel de Molinos supported a mystical approach called Quietism, which presumed the need to sit and wait for the activity of the Holy Spirit, without personal involvement in one's sanctification. His condemnation in 1687, while justifiable, was deadly for mysticism in general. Great clerics like Fenelon were attacked for supporting ideas that could be made to appear to have much in common with Molinos, even when they did not.

℣ Birth of Benito Juarez (1806)
℣ The Failed Second Coming of William Miller (1844)
℣ *L'Action Française* (1908)
℣ Bela Kun and Bolshevik Hungary (1919)

3/22 LEAVE US ALONE DAY

Gallicanism in France and Febronianism in Germany were both eager to assure local bishops independence from Rome. The argument was that this would allow them to operate more in union with local customs. In practice, however, it meant that they were more subject to the desires of the local rulers, local pressures, or whatever it was that the formulators of public opinion in modern society claimed to be essential for the growth of progress.

¶ Arrival of Pius VI in Vienna (1782)
¶ Birth of August Reichensperger (1808), German Catholic leader
¶ Death of Emmanuel Mounier (1950)

3/23 TRY IT, YOU'LL SOIL IT DAY

Jansenists were crypto-Protestants who were convinced that the Jesuit attitude towards consecrating the world to God was corrupting those affected by it. They found numerous ways, both theological as well as pastoral, to teach their message of a simplified religion, based on the wretched condition of mankind.

¶ Hat and Cloak Riots in Spain (1766)
¶ War declared in Austria (1848)
¶ Battle of Novara (1849)
¶ Mussolini's *Fasci di Combattimento* formed (1919)

3/24 BITTER DREGS DAY

The battle of Jansenists versus Jesuits became extremely brutal and bitter, through many episodes from the 1640s onwards. The publication of the papal bull *Unigenitus* (1713) unleashed yet another major war between these factions. The Jansenist journal, *Nouvelles ecclesiastiques*, was a powerful, scandalous propaganda force helping, in the long run, to discredit the Church and also prepare

I. PREPARATION SEASON: MARCH   37

the role of the Press as a primary tool for the formation of public opinion.
¶ Official beginning of the Tokugawa Shogunate (1603)
¶ Death of Jacques Hébert (1794)

3/25 SEE YOU IN COURT DAY

Jansenists had allies in the legal profession, which was itself locked in battle with the royal authority through the aid of the anti-absolutist institutions called *parlements*. The royal authority in France sided with the Papacy against the Jansenists, especially after the bull *Unigenitus* (1713). Jansenists, lawyers and judges then plunged France into endless litigation throughout the course of the 1700s.
¶ Birth of Catherine of Siena (1347)
¶ Birth of Mariano Soler, Archbishop of Montevideo (1846)
¶ Triangle Fire in Greenwich Village (1911)

Thus Endeth INCOHERENT FUMBLING WEEK ■

13 LET THERE BE LIGHT WEEK

Wherein are commemorated enlightened literati who ushered the huddled masses into the light-hearted, free-spirited world of mathematical equations and Bunsen Burners. (1600s–1700s)

3/26 WEIGHING AND MEASURING DAY

Magicians were always looking for the spiritual qualities of material substances in a way that threatened to divinize nature and reintroduce paganism. By the 1600s, many people who were horrified by magic had become convinced that matter had to be treated as something completely separate from spirit so as to avoid this pagan temptation. One way of de-spiritualizing matter was to declare it to be something that could be dealt with by weighing and measuring it alone; something that could be examined on a purely mathematical basis. René Descartes (1596–1650) and Galileo Galilei (1564–1642) took this route.

¶ Execution of François de Charette (1796)
¶ Execution of François Noël Babeuf (1797)
¶ Death of Walt Whitman (1892)
¶ *Estado Nuovo* in Portugal (1933)

3/27 OBSERVATION DAY

Many others, by the same era, had become convinced that the only way that earthly substances could be understood was by means of observing and experimenting with them to find out their true hidden qualities. Francis Bacon (1561–1626) is an example of this second approach towards de-spiritualized matter.

¶ Birth of Franz Xavier von Baader, Catholic political leader (1765)
¶ Death of Edgar Quinet (1875)

3/28 THE MICROCOSM SHALL LIE DOWN WITH THE MACROCOSM DAY

Christianity had convinced the West of the order and purpose of the universe on the one hand, and the freedom and dignity of the individual on the other. Many thinkers simply took these themes for granted, even when they were abandoning their religious beliefs. Hence, they did not see any problems with combining together the idea of an ordered, clock-like universe with the individual demigods that they claimed that universe was supposed to serve.

¶ Frankfurt Assembly decides to offer the Crown of Germany to Prussia (1848)
¶ *Firmissimam constantiam* to Mexican bishops (1937)

3/29 OH WHAT A BEAUTIFUL MORNING DAY

Once the world would be weighed, measured, observed and experimented with by totally free demigods, endless vistas previously unseen would open up to mankind, leading to the construction of the "New Atlantis." Isaac Newton (1642–1727), whatever his own personal doubts about the question, seemed to indicate through his laws of motion that "laws" would soon be found to explain at least almost everything. Galileo and Newton together had shown that both the "sublunary" and the "lunary" world were subject to the same rules.

- Death of the Marquis de Condorcet (1794)
- Ferdinand VII denounces Salic Law (1830)
- Dissolution of the Jesuits in France (1880)
- Spanish Civil War ends (29–30, 1939)

3/30 HOW SHOULD I PROGRESS DAY

Bacon said that "idols", opposed to the totally free use of experimentation and its results, stood in the way of the opening of new vistas. Such "idols" could be summed up in one word: Christianity.

- Birth of Fr. Umberto Benigni, founder of the *Sodalitium Pianum* (1862)
- Poisoning of Archbishop José Ignacio Checa y Barba of Quito (1877)
- Birth of Klaus Schwab (1938)

3/31 USEFUL ICON DAY

Men like Descartes, Galileo and Newton could be held up as practical heroes, opposed to the useless parasites honored by a Church irrationally constructing and maintaining superstitious "idols." The trials of Galileo were a perfect symbol of wisdom persecuted by obscurantism.

- Allies enter Paris (1814)
- US vs. Oregon on Catholic educational freedom (1925)

April

4/1 WHERE THERE'S A WIT, THERE'S A SAVANT DAY

Philosophy and science are one thing; clever writing and propaganda is another. The Enlightenment would not have got very far without the satirical distortions of everyone from Pierre Bayle (1647–1706) through François-Marie Arouet, a.k.a. Voltaire (1694–1778).
- Birth of Joseph de Maistre (1754)
- Flight of General Boulanger from France (1889)
- Emperor Charles I of Austria dies (1922)
- Arrest of Blessed Anacleto González-Flores in Mexico (1926)

Thus Endeth LET THERE BE LIGHT WEEK ■

14 'DAT OLD BLACK MAGIC WEEK

Wherein is commemorated that Catholic irrationality which is clearly demonstrated by Catholic fears concerning irrationality. (1600s–1700s)

4/2 KNOWLEDGE IS POWER DAY

Plato and the Church Fathers believed that knowledge was for the glorification of God. Francis Bacon said that its purpose was for the attainment of power. Obviously, the latter view must be more enlightened and conducive to the progress of mankind, since the wise men of the age simply declared it to be so.

I. PREPARATION SEASON: APRIL 41

℣ Death of Comte de Mirabeau (1791)
℣ Birth of Giacomo Cardinal Antonelli (1806)
℣ Birth of Léon Gambetta (1838)

4/3 IGNORED DIFFICULTY DAY

Philosophes were literary men, the contemporary equivalent of popularizing journalists. They were after a "good argument" rather than scientific accuracy. Hence, they regularly ignored the warnings of men like Isaac Newton that math and science could not really explain everything in the universe through ironclad "laws" which actually served merely as good working hypotheses for action.

℣ "The Black Cardinals" (1810)
℣ Death of Juliusz Slowacki, Polish Romantic poet (1841)
℣ Promulgation of the New "Roman Liturgy" (1969)

4/4 WITCHDOCTOR DAY

Men of Reason said that they were eager for people to believe the testimony of their eyes. Most peoples' eyes told them that the sun went around the earth. The fact that the earth went around the sun made the "observations" of the learned seem to have a kind of "witchdoctor" character about them, turning the scientist into a man whose observations could themselves not be observed by others.

℣ Charlemagne recognized as Emperor by Constantinople (812)
℣ Birth of Dom Prosper Guèranger of Solesmes (1805)

4/5 THE WAR OF THE ANCIENTS AND THE MODERNS DAY

The Enlightenment was made as an alliance between admirers of the classical world and enthusiasts for math and science. Modern math and science far surpassed the achievements of the ancients by the 1600s. Should one, therefore, stick with the old or ring in the new? Such queries augured trouble for the peace of the newly illuminated Magical Kingdom.

¶ Petition of the "Gueux" (1566)
¶ Birth of Thomas Hobbes (1588)
¶ Death of Georges Danton and Camille Desmoulins (1794)
¶ Birth of Jules Ferry (1832)

4/6 IF THIS IS REASON, WHERE IS FAITH DAY

Men of the Enlightenment developed an unquestioning Faith in Reason. Since they had defined themselves as the infallible voice of Reason, anyone who thought them to be in error and sought rational clarification of their confusions had to be a voice of superstitious nonsense and a subject for ridicule rather than reasoning. Hence, the Age of Reason actually ended rational critique of Faith.

¶ Committee of Public Safety (1793)
¶ The foundation of the *Petite Eglise* (1803)
¶ Henry Edward Manning becomes a Catholic (1851)

4/7 YOU'VE GOT SOME NERVE DAY

What was a human individual in the Great Machine of Nature other than a machine part? What was the key to this individual machine? Pierre-Jean-Goerges Cabanis said it was the nerve endings. Clearly, another victory for human dignity!

¶ Birth of Bishop Franz Josef Rudigier of Linz (1811)
¶ Death of Louis Veuillot (1883)

4/8 WHO'S BEHIND THIS DAY

It was, indeed, difficult for Enlightenment thinkers to promote their ideas, at least in the early part of the 1700s. This explains the success of Freemasonry, officially organized from 1717 onwards, and which spread from Britain to the Continent. Many future revolutionary leaders, European and American, became part of Freemasonic lodges.

❡ Birth of Blessed Guillaume J. Chaminade (1761)
❡ Napoleon's Organic Articles (1802)
❡ General silk worker strike in Lyons (1834)

Thus Endeth 'DAT OLD BLACK MAGIC WEEK ■

15 ON THE INSIDE LOOKING OUT WEEK

Wherein is commemorated Modernity's conviction that observation is in the eye of the beholder. Nota especially bene: Those Enlightenment thinkers who placed a greater emphasis on individual freedom than on the ironclad order of the universe began to demonstrate more and more the way in which all judgments about life were affected by personal passions and actions. (1700s)

4/9 YOUR CAUSE HAS NO EFFECT DAY

David Hume (1711–1776), the Scot historian-philosopher, showed that basing scientific "laws" upon observation destroyed all possibility of law, since one could not observe every cause and effect continually for all eternity. "Laws," therefore, involved a leap of faith in the order of the universe, easy enough for the Christian to make, but which people who had abandoned Christianity could simply not justify.

❡ Death of Jacques Necker (1804)
❡ Birth of Charles Pierre Baudelaire (1821)

4/10 I WISH YOU WEREN'T FERTILIZER DAY

Denis Diderot, editor of the *French Encyclopedia* (1751–1777), came to realize that enlightened observation demonstrated the impossible fragmentation of all order under the power of human passion. He was not happy about this, since it destroyed the very faith in beauty with which he, as a literary man, had begun his illuminated search for truth and goodness. But that's life! Even love, ultimately—given human decay—turns out to provide nothing other than fertilizer for a glorious future.

- Death of William of Ockham (1349)
- Solemn Proclamation of the French Concordat (1802)
- *Sacré* of Louis XVIII (1814)
- Death of Teilhard de Chardin (1955)
- Death of Evelyn Waugh (1966)

4/11 NO MORE ANCIENTS JUMPING ON THE BED DAY

A good thing could come out of modern scientific and mathematical discoveries. At least one did not have to live and die in slavish obedience to each and every intellectual and cultural dictate of the Ancient World.

- End of Albigensian Crusade (1229)
- Stresa Front (11–14, 1935)
- Arrest of Cardinal Josyf Slipyi of Lviv (1945)

4/12 I'M PLEASED AS PUNCH TO BE ME DAY

Jean-Jacques Rousseau (1712–1778) showed in his *Confessions* that everyone who stripped himself of his pretensions and hypocrisy, and thus revealed his "natural" character, had to be accepted for what he was. Hence, he himself had to be appreciated as a good man, despite tearing his child away from its mother to send him to

a workhouse. After all, the labor involved in raising the wretched little brat would have rattled his nerves.
- ¶ Capture of Constantinople (1204)
- ¶ Abolition of Mass in Zurich (1525)
- ¶ Dom Christoph Antoine Gerle's Proposal for a Catholic State (1790)
- ¶ French revolutionary bell melting decree (1792)
- ¶ Return of Pius IX to Rome (1850)
- ¶ Death of Franklin Roosevelt (1945)

4/13 YOU'VE GOT TO BE ME DAY

Rousseau "knew" that everyone could be just as honest and perfect as he was, but was stopped from it by mistakenly following the ways of influential external hypocrites. For the world to be natural and good it must, therefore, abandon its hypocrisy and become a carbon copy of the only truly natural man: himself.
- ¶ Edict of Nantes (1598)
- ¶ Civil Constitution condemned by Pope Pius VI (1791)
- ¶ Roman Catholic Relief Bill (1829)
- ¶ Katyn Massacre discovered (1943)

4/14 NOT ME, NOT FREE, CEASE TO BE DAY

Some pathetic souls could not or would not become just like Rousseau. They thus proved themselves to be not only hopelessly enslaved to hypocrisy; they actually demonstrated that they were not even human. Such enemies of mankind must be eliminated for the sake of the wellbeing of mankind as a whole.
- ¶ The Creation of the College of Cardinals (1059)
- ¶ Dagger Day in France (1791)
- ¶ Edict versus the Carbonari in Naples (1814)
- ¶ Departure of King Alfonso XIII from Spain (1931)

4/15 I BELIEVE FOR EVERY DING AN SICH THAT GOES, CONVICTION GROWS

Immanuel Kant (1724–1804) was convinced that outside "reality" could never be known through scientific observation. One could, however, restore universal laws upon the realization that everything the individual believed all people must follow, himself included, just had to be true.

¶ Birth of Fr. Johann Baptist Heinrich, one of the editors of *Der Katholik* (1816)
¶ Birth of Johann Baptist Cardinal Franzelin (1816)
¶ Birth of Bishop Louis Gaston de Ségur (1820)
¶ Foundation of Young Europe (1834)

Thus Endeth ON THE INSIDE LOOKING OUT WEEK ∎

16 DON'T LOOK TOO DEEPLY WEEK

Wherein is commemorated Catholicism's disdain for knowledge, displayed by it worry over the victory of willfulness. (1700s)

4/16 HIDDEN BLESSING DAY

Justice where justice is due! At least Hume and Kant knew there was a problem with basing everything on rational scientific observation.

¶ Battle of Culloden (1746)
¶ Pasque Veronesi (16–17, 1797)
¶ Conversion of Friedrich Schlegel (1809)

4/17 ANYTHING GOES DAY

Still, once the knowledge of cause and effect is denied—thereby preventing the formulation of any natural law—the only thing left to build one's life upon is

I. PREPARATION SEASON: APRIL   47

"custom", separate from any question of truth or goodness. Similarly, the ground for judging what ought to be universally applicable to all men might actually be nothing other than individual willfulness.

¶ Death of Benjamin Franklin (1790)
¶ Birth of Nikita Khrushchev (1894)

4/18 IS THERE REALLY NOTHING WRONG DAY

Here lies the crux of the problem. Is our nature flawed, after Original Sin, or not? If it is flawed, then stripping ourselves down to our "natural desires" and "natural will," or even "time honored customs" may just be a recipe for the victory of evil—and a disaster for us and for all those around us.

¶ Refusal of Luther to reject his heresy before the Emperor Charles V at Worms (1521)
¶ Abolition of Josephism (18–23, 1850)

4/19 I KNOW PARANOIA WHEN I SEE IT DAY

Rousseau's desire to make the whole world a copy of himself in order that it could be honest and natural was accompanied by intense paranoia. Those "enemies of the people" who did not express an interest in becoming Rousseauian clones were, as we have seen, ipso facto condemned as monstrous villains, necessarily destined to destroy the one whole, good man. It was a duel to the death between Rousseau and all hypocritical anti-men. *En garde*, unnatural legions! Your doom is nigh!

¶ The use of the term "Protestants" (1529)
¶ Death of Cardinal Bartolomeo Pacca (1844)
¶ Death of Charles Darwin (1882)
¶ Unification of Nationalist Political Forces in Spain (1937)

4/20 I KNOW PORNOGRAPHY WHEN I SEE IT DAY

Rousseau's ideas, adopted by the myriad of cheap late-eighteenth century journalists, became a justification for the superiority of these mediocre scribblers, who claimed that they were forced, as natural men, to suffer under the hypocrisy of the unnatural outside world. They also allowed for the validation of vulgarity and pornography, which the naturally honest purveyors of rot knew that everyone, in his heart of hearts, was dying to embrace.

- ⁋ French declaration of war against Austria (1792)
- ⁋ Birth of Charles Maurras (1868)
- ⁋ *Humanum genus* on secret societies (1884)

4/21 SIC 'EM DING DAY

Kant argued that it was impossible to know things as they really were. But if there are really *dings* out there that can be known, they will strike back against an individual's distorted, but supposedly "natural" perception of what they are—and destroy him.

- ⁋ Birth of Rome (753 B.C.)
- ⁋ Law vs. refractory priests in France (1792)
- ⁋ Third Carlist War (1872)

4/22 DEAD MEN DON'T BLEED DAY

Individuals' distorted ideas of reality give birth to what is called "ideology," which seeks to bend the reality (which cannot be known) to its will. The results are hell on earth.

- ⁋ Hildebrand elected as Pope Gregory VII (1073)
- ⁋ Birth of Isabella of Castille (1451)
- ⁋ Birth of Vladimir Ulyanov—"Lenin" (1870)
- ⁋ Death of Archbishop José Mora y del Rio of Mexico (1928)

Thus Endeth DON'T LOOK TOO DEEPLY WEEK *and, with it,* PREPARATION SEASON ■

II. ERUPTION SEASON:

"It's Easy if You Try"

(1700'S–1800'S)

17 HAMMER WEEK

Wherein is commemorated a panoply of illuminated forces eager to begin to punish Church and People for their unforgivable flaws. (1700s onwards)

4/23 NOT SO STRANGE BEDFELLOWS DAY

By the middle of the eighteenth century an alliance of anti-Catholic forces was ready to go on the offensive. At first glance, they seemed to be an incoherent group, involving Jansenists, Enlightenment thinkers, civil servants and capitalists. On second glance, it was not so incoherent after all. Indeed, it was simply an updated version of the same forces that had been linked together since the 1200s.

¶ German Beer Purity Law (1516)
¶ Cornerstone laid for El Escorial (1563)
¶ Innocent X against the Jansenists (1654)

4/24 THOSE WHO WORK AND FIGHT DAY

Secularists were interested in earthly improvements that could be weighed and measured. Thus, they were only keen on work and its results. Dynasties around Europe were chiefly interested in the power gained from improved weaponry and economic conditions, brought about by the labors of mathematicians, scientists and other practical men. Britain and Prussia, as we have seen, were the chief objects of admiration of all power seekers.

¶ Battle of Mühlberg (1547)
¶ Dogmatic constitution *Dei Filius* (1870)
¶ Encyclical of Archbishop Errazuriz y Valdivieso of Santiago de Chile (1923)

4/25 WATCH YOUR MANNERS DAY

A focus on practical work and unified national fighting ability was wrecked by disagreements over ideas, especially religious ideas. It was necessary to turn people away from whatever diverted them down such dangerous pathways. What really counted in dealings with one's fellow countrymen was civility and the good manners that would shrink in horror from useless debates and rancor.

¶ Birth of Louis IX (1214)
¶ Catholic Association in Ireland (1823)
¶ Death of Bishop Josef Fessler of Sankt Pölten (1872)

4/26 PUTTING OUT THE CANDLES DAY

Religion wasted so much money that could be diverted to good purposes, like warfare. Hence, the Emperor Joseph II (1780–1790) controlled religious spending, and especially limited candle wax usage.

¶ Petrarch climbs Mount Ventoux (1336)
¶ Florentine Pazzi Conspiracy (1478)
¶ Lay confraternities suppressed in Italy (1806)
¶ Chernobyl (1986)

4/27 NO MORE SITTIN' ON THE STOOP DAY

Religious people also wasted much time in prayers, processions, religious holidays and merriment. This had to stop; productivity demanded it! The Grand Duke Leopold of Tuscany, Joseph II's brother and future Emperor (1790–1792), was one of many philanthropists

introducing reforms cutting back on useful festivities and recreation.
❡ Birth of Edward Gibbon (1737)
❡ Birth of Maurice Baring (1874)
❡ Birth of Guizar Valencia, Bishop of Veracruz (1878)
❡ Antonio de Oliveira Salazar comes into the government in Portugal (1928)

4/28 JESUIT UNDER THE BED DAY

The Jesuits, accused of everything from recruiting a private army in Paraguay to assassinating rulers, were the chief targets of the practical man's disdain. Much effort was spent on destroying the Society of Jesus, beginning with the work of the Kingdom of Portugal (1759).
❡ Pope Clement XII, *In eminenti* versus Freemasons (1738)
❡ Arrest of Bishop Antonio de Macedo Costa of Pará in Brazil (1874)
❡ Birth of Antonio de Oliveira Salazar (1889)
❡ Death of Benito Mussolini (1945)

4/29 UPPING THE ANTE DAY

It was not enough for dynasties to undertake the destruction of the Jesuits on their own steam. They demanded that the Papacy itself join in the kill, and take part in many other secularization measures as well.
❡ Death of Bernardo Tanucci, Italian Enlightenment secularist (1783)
❡ Birth of Archbishop Paul Cardinal Cullen of Armagh/Dublin (1803)
❡ Pope refuses to join the "Holy War" versus Austria (1848)

Thus Endeth HAMMER WEEK ∎

18 ANVIL WEEK

Wherein is commemorated the Catholics' compounding of their crimes by trying different means of protecting themselves. (1700s)

4/30 TRY AND TRY AGAIN DAY

The seventeenth and eighteenth centuries were replete with efforts on the part of Church authorities to fend off the assault on the supernatural in the name of pure power politics and practicality.

¶ Dissolution of the National Guard in France (1827)
¶ Caroline de Bourbon in Marseilles (1832)
¶ Lamennais' *Les Paroles d'un croyant* (1834)

May

5/1 RECRUITMENT SERGEANT DAY

A sign of the Papacy's weakness in this regard was its inability to fend off forcible recruitment of soldiers by the Great Powers in the Papal States and in Rome itself.

¶ Birth of Fr. Bernard Overberg (1754)
¶ Birth of Archbishop Thomas Cardinal Gousset of Rheims (1792)
¶ Birth of Teilhard de Chardin (1881)
¶ New Hampshire issues liquor licenses (1903)
¶ *The Catholic Worker* (1933)

5/2 I WISH I WERE IN COENA DAY

The Papacy complained of abuses by governments in a bull every Holy Thursday called *In coena*.

¶ Death of St. Antoninus of Florence (1459)
¶ The *Dos de Mayo* Rising vs. Napoleon (1808)
¶ Birth of Fr. Carlo Passaglia, S.J. (1812)

5/3 KEEP YOUR MOUTH SHUT DAY

The last thing that dynasties wanted was to hear recriminations. Hence, the many attempts made in the name of their "honor" to end the practice of *In coena*. These were ultimately successful under Pope Clement XIV in 1770.

¶ Birth of Machiavelli (1469)
¶ Fifth Lateran Council (1512)
¶ Louis XVIII's entry into Paris (1814)
¶ Anarchist revolt in Barcelona (3–10, 1937)

5/4 PRAISING THOSE THAT KILL YOU DAY

But why stop with a mere imposition of silence. Better to get one's victim to express approval of being victimized! The reign of Pope Clement XIV (1769–1774) was one long expression of pleased as punch papal self-humiliation.

¶ Five Carthusians from Charterhouse in London hung, drawn and quartered (1535)

¶ Birth of Horace Mann (1796)

¶ Ferdinand VII re-establishes full monarchical rule in Spain (1814)

5/5 NO LAND IN SIGHT DAY

The Jesuits were deported from their missionary centers and, if they were lucky, from Portugal and Spain as well, starting in 1759. Those that stayed were often imprisoned under miserable conditions. Those that embarked found that no country wanted them to disembark. Many were stranded on the high seas for some time.

¶ Events leading to Pope Formosus trial (896)

¶ Opening of Estates General (1789)

¶ Birth of Soren Kierkegaard (1813)

¶ Death of Napoleon (1821)

¶ Birth of the Baron von Hügel (1852)

¶ Garibaldi sails for Sicily (1860)

¶ Anticlerical laws in Spain (1931)

5/6 POINTLESS TRAVEL DAY

Pope Pius VI (1775–1799) tried to fight off Josephism by taking a trip to complain of secularizing measures directly to the Emperor himself in Vienna (1782). It achieved little.

¶ The Fall and Sack of Rome (1527)

II. ERUPTION SEASON: MAY

❡ Death of Bishop Cornelius Jansen (1638)
❡ Fr. Adolf Kolping's first Association (1849)
❡ Birth of Juan Donoso Cortes (1809)

Thus Endeth ANVIL WEEK ∎

19 TERROR WEEK

Wherein is commemorated the French Revolution's simultaneous reprimanding of the past for having put obstacles in its path, for having nevertheless prepared it, and for having ever existed at all. (1700s)

5/7 OLD TIME ALLIANCE DAY

The medieval alliance of heretics, capitalists, and those eager for a strengthening of centralized, bureaucratic government was clearly active as a main long-term cause of the French Revolution. The government of the *Ancièn Régime* was still too Catholic, too economically diverse, and too weak to be acceptable to it.

❡ Second Council of Lyons opens (1274)
❡ Decree establishing the Cult of Supreme Being (1794)
❡ Franz Josef celebrates his Golden Jubilee (1908)

5/8 I AM NOT WHAT I AM DAY

Men think of the French Revolution as leading to a victory for "the People." It was actually a victory for a quite small number of moneymen, one of whose first actions was to end the democratic voting that elected the Estates-General. This was replaced by a highly restricted vote based on property worth, and a still more restricted access to office based on a yet greater personal wealth.

❡ The Act of Uniformity (1559)
❡ Death of the Marquis de Pombal (1782)

❡ Death of the Duke de Choiseul (1785)
❡ Antoine Lavoisier guillotined (1794)
❡ Death of Oswald Spengler (1936)

5/9 WHO'S IN CHARGE DAY

France was not used to be being ruled by a National Assembly. Cities organized their own municipal governments, backed by their own National Guards. The Paris Commune, in effect, took the King and National Assembly prisoner, bringing them from Versailles to the capital and leaving open to the rest of the country the question of who was actually responsible for national affairs.

❡ Athanasius is elected Patriarch of Alexandria (328)
❡ Duke Henri de Guise's troops occupy Paris (1588)
❡ FCC Chairman Newton N. Minow criticizes television as a "vast wasteland" (1961)

5/10 BOTTOM'S UP DAY

Paris was a center for political clubs, election ward shenanigans, and smutty political journalism. All manner of men who would never have had a chance to influence politics under the *Ancièn Régime* were now able to crawl out of the woodwork to take advantage of a shaky new set of institutions. Their only serious competitors were the omnipresent capitalists who nevertheless cooperated with them, since they, too, had gained from the Revolution. The moneymen did not exactly know how to operate in the world of political ideology or what this buddy system would bring about in the long run.

❡ Meeting of the Abbot de St. Cyran and Jansenius (1623)
❡ The Battle of Lodi (1796)
❡ Failure of Babeuf's Conspiracy (1796)

II. ERUPTION SEASON: MAY

5/11 I NEVER DID LIKE DAD DAY

The Revolution became an assault on everything that retained a trace of the supernatural and truly diverse past of France. All of this magnificent heritage had to be destroyed — along with the bones of the Kings buried at St. Denis, which were exhumed and dispersed by the new lovers of mankind.

¶ Death of Fr. Matteo Ricci (1610)
¶ Death of Archbishop Jean-Siffrein Cardinal Maury of Paris (1817)
¶ May Laws (11–14, 1873)
¶ Birth of Fr. Philip Hughes (1895)

5/12 INELUCTABLE LOGIC DAY

"Will power" being the only determinant of thought and ethics left to guide modern man, the Revolution swiftly fell into the hands of the most willful of all of its supporters. Men like Maximilien Robespierre (1758–1794) spoke eloquently of the need to move ever more logically (i.e., willfully) to the creation of a new kind of virtuous citizen.

¶ The Day of Barricades in Paris (1588)
¶ The end of the Republic of Venice (1797)
¶ Catholic Association in Ireland (1823)
¶ Death of Luigi Cardinal Lambruschini (1854)
¶ Death of J.K. Huysmans (1907)

5/13 YOUR DEFENSE IS MY OFFENSE DAY

Disagreements in the ranks of the revolutionaries became more severe by 1794. Purges reached insane proportions. In classic Rousseauian fashion, the mere act of defending oneself would be proclaimed proof of hypocrisy by the strongest of the strong.

¶ Birth of Pius IX (1792)

58   A CAUTIONARY CALENDAR

❡ Birth of Alexei Khomiakov (1804)
❡ Law of Guarantees in Italy (1871)
❡ First Fatima Apparition (1917)

Thus Endeth TERROR WEEK ■

20 BRING OUT YOUR DEAD WEEK

Wherein is commemorated Catholic discovery of the disadvantages of being free, equal and fraternal. (1700s)

5/14 TREASON OF THE CLERKS DAY

The clergy itself was involved in the Enlightenment and then in revolutionary activities, from the calling of the Estates-General through until the fall of Robespierre. A case is point is Bishop Talleyrand-Périgord (1754–1838), who abandoned his clerical state, voted for the death of the King, and built himself an extremely successful secular career.

❡ Coronation of Charles VIII, The Affable (1483)
❡ François Ravaillac murders Henry IV (1610)
❡ We Want Beer Parade in New York (1932)

5/15 SOMEONE'S GOT TO PAY DAY

The primary practical reason for the beginning of the Revolution was the government's bankruptcy. No one wanted to pay extra taxes. Nationalizing and then selling the property of the Church in 1789, using the justification that that property existed for the sake of the common good, got everybody else off the hook.

❡ Emperor flees Vienna (1848)
❡ Victory of Garibaldi in Sicily (1860)
❡ Law of Guarantees refused by the Holy See (1871)
❡ *Rerum novarum* (1891)
❡ *Quadragesimo anno* (1931)

II. ERUPTION SEASON: MAY

5/16 PRIESTLY PEOPLE DAY

Jansenists had grown more and more eager for a "democratic" Church in the course of the 1700s. Secularists wanted to democratize the Church to destroy its canonical character and ties with Rome. The Civil Constitution of the Clergy (1790) achieved all three goals simultaneously.

¶ Baldwin IX, Count of Flanders, crowned Latin Emperor of Constantinople (1204)

¶ Marshal MacMahon's attempted "coup" (1877)

5/17 UNEXPECTED TRAVEL DAY

Almost every bishop, as well as half of the clergy, refused to accept the Oath to the Civil Constitution of the Clergy. Most fled the country between 1790 and 1794. Pius VI himself died while being carried off into exile in 1799.

¶ French Annexation of Papal States (1809)

¶ *Commissum Divinitas* (1835) on Church and State in Switzerland

¶ Death of Charles Maurice de Talleyrand (1838)

5/18 DESECRATION DAY

The so-called "Enraged Ones" began a full-scale attack on religion in 1792, their most famous actions involving desecrating cemeteries and rededicating Churches to secular purposes. Former priests often led such activities.

¶ Fall of Acre (1291)

¶ Call for burning of book of Nicholas of Autrecourt (1346, done 1347)

¶ Death of Pietro Pompanazzi (1525)

¶ Frankfurt Assembly (1848)

¶ Birth of Bertrand Russell (1872)

5/19 UP TO ONE'S NECK IN WATER DAY

The Catholic population of the *Vendée* could not endure the attack on the Church or the revolutionary universal draft. The Republic crushed the *Vendée* in 1793 and undertook the first genocide in history. One of its most cruel butcheries were the *Noyades* (Drownings) of Nantes.

¶ Anne Boleyn beheaded (1536)
¶ Birth of Johann Gottlieb Fichte (1762)

5/20 IS THIS THE EVENING OF THE DAY DAY

Revolutionaries hailed the death of Pope Pius VI in Valence on the way to a French prison in 1799 as the end of "The Infamous Thing." Perhaps many Catholics thought the Papacy had reached the end of the line as well.

¶ Wounding of Ignatius of Loyola (1521)
¶ Beginning of the "White Terror" in France (1795)
¶ Birth of Honoré de Balzac (1799)
¶ Birth of John Stuart Mill (1806)

Thus Endeth BRING OUT YOUR DEAD WEEK ■

21 ORDER IN THE COURTROOM WEEK

Wherein is commemorated the world turned upside down, suffering vertigo by illogically trying to set itself right again and climb to former heights. (1800s)

5/21 SELF-MADE MAN DAY

Napoleon (1769–1821) was a man of order who, nevertheless, could never have "made it" in France without the shake-up caused by the Revolution. Therefore, he tried to combine order and tradition on the one hand with revolutionary novelty on the other. Ultimately, the sole reliable pillar of his power was the army.

II. ERUPTION SEASON: MAY

- Birth of King Philip II of Spain (1527)
- Birth of Joseph Fouché, Napoleon's police chief (1759)
- Bloody Week in Paris begins (1871)
- Death of Jane Addams (1935)

5/22 BLESS THEM ALL DAY

The Church tried to work with whatever regime would give it some space to operate. Hence, it accepted the Concordat with Napoleon in 1801.

- Death of Victor Hugo (1885)
- Comintern abolished (1943)

5/23 BUSINESS AS USUAL DAY

"Legitimist" governments claimed that everything would work out well so long as there were a "return to normalcy"; i.e., to the rule of the monarchies legally in power in 1789.

- Execution of Savonarola (1498)
- Election of Carafa as Paul IV (1555)
- Defenestration of Prague (1618)
- Birth of Fr. Theodosius Florentini, Swiss Capuchin (1808)
- Death of J.D. Rockefeller (1937)

5/24 RUSSIAN ROULETTE DAY

One of these Legitimist governments was also Russia. Its Emperor, Alexander I, claimed to wish to protect Christianity versus the Revolution. Some nineteenth century Catholics dreamed that the Orthodox Russian Empire would convert and lead all of Europe back to the True Faith. The Papacy was more dubious.

- Return of Pius VII to Rome (1814)
- Birth of Valère Fallon, SJ (1875)
- Birth of Bob Dylan (1941)

5/25 CHECK AND BALANCE DAY

Perhaps the Liberal, English-style governments, which came to power in countries like Belgium, might also prove to be beneficial to the Church's cause? This, too, was the dream of many believers in the 1830s and 1840s.

¶ Death of Gregory VII (1085)
¶ Edict of Worms (1521)
¶ First National Synod in France (1559)
¶ Birth of Ralph Waldo Emerson (1803)
¶ Death of Émile Combes (1921)

5/26 JUSTE MILIEU DAY

France gained a liberal government in 1830 under Louis-Philippe (1830–1848), and one that claimed an interest in prudent, non-violent change. Might this be a working partner, too?

¶ Flight of Michael of Cesena and William of Ockham (1328)
¶ Pope Pius X publishes *Editae saepe*: the "Borromeo Encyclical" irritating German Protestants (1910)
¶ Birth of Jack Kevorkian (1928)

5/27 I'VE SHOT THEM ALL DAY

Army officers, following the Bonapartist coup d'état route, took over power in various countries, in the Iberian Peninsula and South America in particular. Might they be tradition-friendly?

¶ Death of Thomas Müntzer (1525)
¶ Death of Jean Calvin (1564)
¶ Refractory priests deported (1792)

Thus Endeth ORDER IN THE COURTROOM WEEK ■

22 NO CATHOLICS NEED APPLY WEEK

Wherein is commemorated Catholic grasping of the modern virtue of trusting no one. (1800s)

5/28 THRONE AND GROAN DAY

Legitimist governments everywhere were "pro-Christian"—so long as the Christians understood that their mission was to defend the status quo and go no further. In Russia, pro-Christian did not mean pro-Catholic, even in Catholic areas like Poland. Eastern Catholicism was prohibited almost entirely.

¶ Birth of August Reichensperger (1810)
¶ Death of Bishop Grégoire (1831)
¶ End of the Paris Commune (1871)
¶ Portuguese coup d'état (1926)
¶ Death of Marc Sangnier (1950)

5/29 CLOSE THE DOOR, LOCK THE KEY DAY

Being a zealous bishop could prove to be a recipe for a legitimist prison sentence, as Bishop von Droste-zu Vischering of Cologne came to realize from 1836–1840.

¶ Fall of Constantinople (1453)
¶ Birth of G.K. Chesterton (1874)

5/30 SCHOOL'S OUT DAY

But, golly gosh, Liberal governments were no better! They especially despised Catholic schooling, particularly on the secondary and university level. Yes, that kind of education was still presumed to be all right for little children. After all, the sole learning the cherubs required—the offspring of the lower classes most of all—was that of just how wicked it was to steal bourgeois property.

¶ Arrest of Pasquier Quesnel (1703)

¶ Birth of Mikhail Bakunin (1814)

¶ Death of Archbishop Emmanuel Cardinal Suhard of Paris (1949)

5/31 LITTLE BROTHERS DAY

The 1830s were the season for the destruction of the Franciscans and Dominicans at the hands of the Liberal government of Spain.

¶ Emperor Maximilian, Pope Alexander VI, Milan, King Ferdinand, Isabella & Venice sign anti-French Holy League (1495)

¶ Pope Innocent X's *Cum occasione* against the Jansenists (1653)

¶ Frederick II ascends throne of Prussia (1740)

June

6/1 JESUITS UNDER THE BED AGAIN DAY

Liberal professors like Jules Michelet and Edgar Quinet, in their courses in Paris in 1843, taught that the Jesuits were at it again, trying to prevent prudent Progress. Jesuits had to learn to change homes regularly, and their own prudence often dictated their leaving town before being thrown out. They also had to resign themselves to seeing themselves ridiculed in cheap novels.

- Emperor Didius Julianus is assassinated (193)
- Pope Pius II opens the Congress of Mantua (1459)
- Duke of Alba oversees the beheading of 18 nobles in Brussels (1568)
- Death of John Dewey (1952)

6/2 YOU JUST CAN'T WIN DAY

Catholics discovered that participation in liberal government did not mean that they were allowed to benefit from it. When Catholic candidates won election, they were often excluded from taking office, since they did not share "the right spirit." The Kingdom of Sardinia was particularly unpleasant in this regard.

- The Marquis De Sade's birth (1740)
- Gordon Riots (10 days, 1780)
- Girondin overthrown (1793)
- Birth of Pope Pius X (1835)
- Birth of Emile Mâle (1862)

6/3 YOU ARE BLACK BUT BEAUTIFUL DAY

Still, perhaps the Church could be considered acceptable if she came to learn that the seed of her message had been preserved and developed in birth after rebirth—through what was called *palingenesis*—until now, when it was finally represented at its best: by Liberalism.

¶ Birth of Jefferson Davis (1808)
¶ Émile Combes in power in France (1902)
¶ Chinese Government begins crackdown in Tiananmen Square (1989)

Thus Endeth NO CATHOLICS NEED APPLY WEEK ■

23 YOU SHOULD HAVE BEEN AN ACCOUNTANT WEEK

Wherein is commemorated the first presentation of an abundant supply of materialist demands to the under-productive and under-consuming masses. (1800s)

6/4 ACTIVE CITIZEN DAY

The French Revolution defined citizenship on the basis of property ownership. The richer that one was, the more "active" as opposed to "passive" his citizenship could be.

¶ Robespierre elected President of the National Convention (1794)
¶ The Constitution *octroyé* of Louis XVIII (1814)
¶ Battle of Magenta (1859)
¶ Death of Maurice Blondel (1949)

6/5 WANT A JOB DAY

With the Industrial Revolution, salaried employment became more and more the norm. The ability to keep passive citizens alive fell into the hands of their active

II. ERUPTION SEASON: JUNE   67

compatriots, who were deeply concerned that they get enough physical exercise and stay slim and trim, so as to build their characters.

¶ Birth of Adam Smith (1723)
¶ Birth of Fr. John-Joseph Gaume (1802)
¶ Social Riots in Paris (1832)

6/6 SPEED 'EM UP DAY

Trains made transportation faster, allowing for a swifter supplying of ever more heated consumption. People working in factories had to speed up their production as well. Otherwise, the trains would not be happy.

¶ Death of Jeremy Bentham (1832)
¶ Death of the Count Camillo Benso di Cavour (1861)
¶ Catholic victory in Belgium (1880)

6/7 BEAUTIFUL IS EXPENDABLE DAY

Utilitarianism became a standard philosophy for the speed 'em up generation. And Utilitarianism had no time for any idea of beauty that was not practical and materially productive. Jeremy Bentham (1748–1832) is one of Utilitarianism's most famous proponents. You can still visit him, pickled, at University College, London.

¶ First Crusaders arrive at the fortifications of Jerusalem (1099)
¶ Field of the Cloth of Gold (1520)
¶ Louis XIV crowned (1654)
¶ Anti-Catholic riots in London (1780)
¶ Lateran Accords (1929)

6/8 CHELSEA LIVING ROOM DAY

And Utilitarianism was so efficient! Once you knew exactly how mechanically predictable people were, you could foresee how everyone would act anywhere in the universe. Hence, Jeremy Bentham's comment that he could legislate for all of India without leaving his home in London.

¶ Birth of Ercole Cardinal Consalvi (1757)
¶ Death of Thomas Paine (1809)
¶ Death of Jean Paul de Villeneuve-Bargemont (1850)
¶ Death of Gerard Manley Hopkins (1889)
¶ Emily Davidson dies happily of her own free will at the race track (1913)

6/9 BIGGER AND BETTER WEAPONS DAY

Existing governments might not be thrilled with industrialization in and of itself. But supporting it gained such beautiful new weaponry! Being prepared for war meant opening the doors to the fresh winds of capitalism.

¶ Congress of Vienna ends (1815)
¶ Gregory XVI's *Cum primum* on the revolt in Poland (1832)

6/10 HOMOGENIZATION DAY

It was already becoming clear in the early 1800s that each step in the path of industrialization generated further mechanization and standardization. But would these "black, satanic mills" homogenize everything lovely out of existence?

¶ Frederick Barbarossa drowns on the way to the Holy Land (1190)
¶ Arrest of Thomas Cromwell (1540)
¶ Prairial Laws (1794)
¶ Excommunication of Napoleon (1809)

Thus Endeth YOU SHOULD HAVE BEEN AN ACCOUNTANT WEEK ■

24 BROTHER CAN YOU SPARE A DIME WEEK

Wherein are commemorated the lamentation offered and the penance done by the consumption-challenged for their unforgivable failure to purchase. (1800s)

6/11 IS THAT ALL THERE IS DAY

Romanticism complained that the mechanist mentality did not grasp the mystery and the diversity of human life. It was not possible to build a decent civilization on utilitarian pillars, because these only gave scope for the recognition of half of the human personality—and that half, the lower half.

¶ Basilica of St. Denis is dedicated (1144)
¶ Death of Prince Klemens von Metternich (1859)
¶ Pius X's *Il fermo proposito* (1905)

6/12 ROOM FOR A VIEW DAY

Space had to be allowed for the non-utilitarian to thrive. Hence, Charles Dickens' Sissy in *Hard Times,* who understood that the definition of a horse was not exhausted by a recounting of the number of its teeth, but by the realization of how its use by a masterful rider ennobled both the animal and the man.

¶ Edward VI accepts Cranmer's Forty Two Articles (1553)
¶ Comte François de Montlosier's *Memoires* placed on the Index (1826)
¶ Beginnings of the liberal revolt in Belgium (1846)

6/13 SCRAPS FROM THE TABLE DAY

What did the workingman get from industrialization? Bad housing, miserable working conditions, isolation from traditional community life, and terrible boredom to boot. No matter! Proper economic education would demonstrate that, given the right circumstances, and by doing violence to his soul, one out of a thousand among them might also be placed in a position where he, too, could exploit his fellow men and former comrades.

¶ Martin Luther's marriage (1525)
¶ Birth of Étienne Gilson (1884)

6/14 POOR BUT HAPPY DAY

Poverty was one thing; pauperism quite another. Dom Giacomo Margotti, active in Italy in the middle of the nineteenth century, in a book entitled *Rome and London Compared*, showed that many poor people survived in "backward" Italy with their human dignity intact, while industrialized London saw the poor transformed into paupers who immeasurably worsened poverty by living it out in a hopelessly atomistic and inhuman culture.

¶ The Capitulary of Querzy (877)
¶ Cardinal Ruffo captures Naples (1799)
¶ Battle of Marengo (1800)
¶ Birth of Che Guevara (1928)
¶ Death of G.K. Chesterton (1936)

6/15 CHICAGO FIRE DAY

One of the bizarre features of industrial capitalism was that it made money off of everything. In fact, stability and happiness caused a counterproductive satiety leading to limited consumption. Disaster could prime the pump of the economy much better, reconstruction bringing with it more work and more profits.

¶ *Exsurge Domine* (1520)
¶ Nuncio ordered out of Portugal (1760)
¶ Augustin Bonnetty's ideas attacked in the Four Propositions (1855)
¶ *Eximiam tuam* vs Anton Günther (1857)

II. ERUPTION SEASON: JUNE

6/16 DON'T COMPROMISE, ORGANIZE DAY

It was inevitable that there would be reaction against the position into which workingmen had been thrown by industrialism. One obvious reaction took the form of the unionization of labor.

¶ Jean-Baptiste de Martignac turns against the Jesuits (1828)

¶ Pius IX elected (1846)

¶ Death of Archbishop Henri Louis Charles Maret, Liberal Catholic hero (1884)

6/17 INEVITABLE ANGER DAY

Various forms of Socialism, ill defined, inchoate, and often in conflict with one another, were yet another form of reaction to abuse. Some of these could become violent, as the riots in Paris in 1848, fueled by desperation in the midst of economic crisis, demonstrated.

¶ Call for the Estates General to become the National Assembly (1789)

¶ Forced resignation of Cardinal Consalvi (1806)

¶ *De Tijd* (1845), Dutch Catholic Journal

Thus Endeth BROTHER CAN YOU SPARE A DIME WEEK ■

25 THE MORE THE MERRIER WEEK

Wherein is commemorated the flourishing of the banner of democracy from ever more dizzying heights and vistas. (1800s)

6/18 GIVE ME FIVE MINUTES MORE DAY

Democrats argued that Robespierre was prevented from establishing the Republic of Virtue just as it was at its moment of fruition. Would that he (and the guillotine) had had just a tiny bit more time to finish the job at hand. With the right victims!

¶ Rus Vikings attack Constantinople (860)
¶ States of Utrecht forbid Catholic worship (1580)
¶ Birth of Theophan Prokopovich (1681)
¶ Waterloo (1815)
¶ General Luigi Pelloux resigns as Prime Minister of Italy (1900)

6/19 BIG ROCK CANDY MOUNTAIN DAY

The natural man, as Rousseau had demonstrated, was a fount of goodness. Who could doubt the heights that would be climbed and the benefits that would be accumulated once the natural goodness of the People in general was tapped and set to work?

¶ Sir Robert Peel introduces Metropolitan Police Act (1829)
¶ Execution of Emperor Maximillian (1867)
¶ Death of Lord John Acton (1902)
¶ Dollfuss bans Nazi Party in Austria (1933)

6/20 SILENT MAJORITY DAY

The Abbé Félicité de la Mennais, (more commonly rendered "Lamennais") (1782–1854) was one of those who, in the Catholic ranks, was also convinced of the supreme merit of the People. He reached this conclusion, to begin with, from a counterrevolutionary standpoint, by noting that the People had been most opposed to the ravages of the radicals against religion and the old monarchy. Did this not prove that they formed a reliable silent majority on which the Truth could firmly count for support?

¶ Iconoclasm in Zurich (June 20–July 2, 1524)
¶ Tennis Court Oath (1789)
¶ The Flight to Varennes (20–21, 1791)
¶ Mob invades the Tuilleries (1792)

- ❡ "Peace" in Italy (1797)
- ❡ Death of Abbé Emmanuel Joseph Sièyes (1836)
- ❡ Leo XIII's *Libertas* (1888)

6/21 MYSTICAL ENERGY DAY

Lamennais, as a Catholic, was also convinced that this goodness and truthfulness of the People proved that the Holy Spirit was working through them. The Holy Spirit's work was particularly clear when the People manifested thrilling vibrancy and energy in their actions.

- ❡ Birth of Swiss Guards (1505)
- ❡ Birth of J.P. Sartre (1905)
- ❡ Arreglos in Mexico betraying the Cristeros (1929)

6/22 CONSCIOUSNESS RAISING DAY

Alas! The Silent Majority was just that—silent! It lacked the thrilling vibrancy and energy that it needed to display to prove that the Holy Spirit was behind it. What it needed was to be pushed by a Vanguard of the People to express more enthusiastically what it must surely think. Who better to express the true wishes of the Silent Majority than an already energetic prophet like the good Abbé?

- ❡ Death of Bishop John Fisher of Rochester (1535)
- ❡ Birth of Bishop Joseph Ludwig Colmar of Mainz (1760)
- ❡ Birth of Giuseppe Mazzini (1805)
- ❡ June Days begin in Paris (1848)

6/23 ACT OF FAITH DAY

Was one not convinced of this truth regarding The Prophet of Democracy? How could that be possible since the Holy Spirit had clearly spoken! Obviously, an act of Faith was required for a full understanding of the mystery. O ye reactionary Catholics of little Faith!

- ❡ Icelandic Parliament established (930)
- ❡ Program of King (1789)
- ❡ Banishment of both the Bonapartists and the Orleanists (1886)
- ❡ Brexit Referendum (2016)

6/24 PALINGENESIS DAY

Democrats of many stripes who did not wish to condemn the entire western past also adopted the argument that the seed of the Christian message had fallen into the soil on a number of occasions, appearing to have died, only to be reborn again in new and more glorious forms. The discovery that the infallible voice of the Holy Spirit was to be heard through the prophetic message of charismatic energizers of the People made them realize that this was Christianity's latest and most democratic perfect form of expression.

- ❡ Field of Lies (833)
- ❡ Foundation of the Grand Lodge of England (1717)
- ❡ Battle of Solferino (1859)

Thus Endeth THE MORE THE MERRIER WEEK ∎

26 THE ONE IS NOT THE MANY WEEK

Wherein is commemorated the democratic love of what turns out to be masquerade balls. (1800s)

6/25 SHALL WE DANCE DAY

Legitimist governments had not proven to be necessarily reliable from the Church's point of view. Liberalism had not created an exactly brilliant record for itself either. Perhaps the Church ought to try her luck with democracy? Maybe reliance on the Silent Majority would prove to be more effective!

II. ERUPTION SEASON: JUNE

¶ Fall of the Anabaptist Paradise in Münster (1535)
¶ Gregory XVI's *Singulari nos* (1834)
¶ Death of Archbishop Denise-August Affre of Paris (1848)

6/26 WHAT GOES UP MAY NOT COME DOWN DAY

Democracy proved to be a difficult tool. After all, it needed to be interpreted, by its prophets, in the "right spirit." Perhaps the People would never match the prophets' expectations? Perhaps they would never see things in the right spirit? Why, perhaps the silent People would never become the energetic People after all? Thankfully, orthodox Catholicism had never thought the People were infallible to begin with. Still, the People did exist, and their right to existence as something other than a plaything of Prophets was sacrosanct.

¶ Death of Julian the Apostate (363)
¶ Luther's Debate with Eck (through to July, 1519)
¶ Birth of Jean Siffrein Cardinal Maury (1746)

6/27 THE STATE IS NOT THE CHURCH DAY

Lamennais had been angry with Legitimist governments for interfering with the life of the Church. Hence, he wanted a separation of Church and State. Unfortunately, everything that he claimed to be "spiritual" required much more political activity and submission from the State than ever before in Catholic History. What one got from Lamennais was a charismatic, democratic Church-State that fraudulently called itself a secular government.

¶ Flora MacDonald helps Bonnie Prince Charlie escape (1746)
¶ Louis XVI orders the other Estates to join the National Assembly (1789)
¶ Death of Wenzel von Kaunitz (1794)

6/28 CHAMELEON DAY

What, really, did the People think, even supposing that it was truly the People's voice that was being heard and not that of its elitist Prophets and interpreters? Could its thoughts change from day to day, and Truth and Morality along with them? Could murdering one's grandmother be bad yesterday—if a majority believed so—and good today—if that same majority changed its mind?

- ¶ Birth of Jean-Jacques Rousseau (1712)
- ¶ Birth of Fr. Fredrick William Faber (1814)
- ¶ Assassination of the Archduke Franz Ferdinand (1914)

6/29 DIALOGUE DAY

Pius IX (1846–1878) was ready to admit that a little good will could go a long way. Hence, he began his reign in 1846 with a call for dialogue, with democrats included in it.

- ¶ Birth of Giacomo Leopardi (1798)
- ¶ Pius IX's *Aeterni patris* summoning Vatican One (1868)
- ¶ Leo XIII's *Diuturnum illud* on politics (1881)
- ¶ Leo XIII's *Satis cognitum* (1896)
- ¶ Pius XI's *Non abbiamo bisogno* (1931)
- ¶ Pius XII's *Mystici corporis* (1943)

6/30 I THINK I MADE A BLUNDER DAY

Things did not work out as Pius IX hoped that they might. The "hidden agenda" of the charismatic prophets of democracy, rejecting the Catholic will of an already existing majority, became much more clear and much more ominous. It was time for a change of trajectory.

- ¶ Cardinal Albornoz appointed to clean up the Papal States in Italy (1353)
- ¶ Birth of Adam Müller (1779)
- ¶ Prayer after Mass for Russia (1930)
- ¶ Holy Office *Monitum* versus Teilhard de Chardin (1962)

July

7/1 SHALL WE PARTY DAY

If Parliaments were going to be elected, and large numbers of people were going to vote, would it not be better for Catholics to organize political parties to push an acceptable program of their own? Would they not thus allow for the expression of a true majority will?

- Permission for Jesuits to stay in France (1565)
- First issue of *L'Osservatore Romano* (1861)
- Death of Bakunin (1876)
- Spanish Pastoral Letter in support of the Nationalists (1937)

Thus Endeth THE ONE IS NOT THE MANY WEEK ■

27 LOVE IT OR LEAVE IT WEEK

Wherein is commemorated the burying of different nations' heads in infertile soil. (1800s)

7/2 EACH HIS OWN DAY

Romantic thinkers, themselves emerging out of the Enlightenment context, began to argue that every ethnic group was so different, one from the other, that each had its own specific way of understanding truth, goodness and beauty.

- Death of Jean Jacques Rousseau (1778) — What else could possibly count?
- Perhaps the birth of Herman Hesse (1877)

7/3 STIRRING UP DAY

God had created each distinct ethnic group as it was. To understand the puzzle of the universe, each piece had to deliver its particular message. It could not do so unless it were united and made politically free. Each and every nation had to come together and gain independence.

⁋ Hugh Capet elected (987)
⁋ Return of Pius VII to Rome (1800)
⁋ French enter Rome (1849)
⁋ Battle of Sadowa (1866)
⁋ Pius X's *Lamentabili* (1907)

7/4 BE THAT WHICH IS BECOMING DAY

There were as yet no Germans or Italians since they had no united nation. In order to be true Germans and Italians, one had to cease to be what everyone thought was a German or Italian up until the current moment in time. Unfortunately, the new, truly "real" Germans and Italians, all tended to look exactly the same as modern, liberal or democratic Englishmen or Frenchmen.

⁋ The Horns of Hattin (1187)
⁋ Redemption of the Human Race begins in the American Colonies (1776)
⁋ Birth of Garibaldi (1807)
⁋ Law versus Religious Orders in Germany (1872)

7/5 DEUS LO VULT DAY

Since God stands behind the creation of independent nations, anything that is done to bring them into being forwards God's will; anything that is done to prevent their creation involves alliance with the Evil One.

⁋ *Laetantur Caeli* on Union with the Greeks (1439)
⁋ Foundation of the Nine Sisters Lodge (1776)
⁋ Salazar becomes Prime Minister of Portugal (1932)

II. ERUPTION SEASON: JULY

7/6 POLES APART DAY

No one was more convinced of the support of God in its creation as an independent nation than Polish revolutionaries, many of whose spokesmen were in exile in Paris. Poland, especially Russian Poland, became the image of the suffering, Christ-Nation; its nationalists, prophets of a better world to come.

- ¶ Death of Thomas More (1535)
- ¶ Gustavus Adolphus lands in the Holy Roman Empire to fight in Thirty Years War (1630)
- ¶ The Martyrs of Orange (6–26, 1794)
- ¶ Birth of Archbishop Karl Cardinal von Reisach of Freising/Munich (1800)
- ¶ Deportation of Pius VII (1809)

7/7 THIS IS THE MOMENT DAY

1848 saw nationalist movements bursting into violence in Italy, Germany and Hungary. Attempts were made to use the opportunity to unify all of them.

- ¶ Pragmatic Sanction of Bourges (1438)
- ¶ Chocolate introduced to Europe (1550)
- ¶ Abraham Kuyper victory in Netherlands (1901)

7/8 WHAT ABOUT ME DAY

None of these movements succeeded at the time, although most of Italy was united by 1861, much of Germany in 1871, and Hungary given equal status with Austria in 1867. But what was one to do about the other ethnic nationalities in Europe? Did God not want them to create and fit into their piece of the divine puzzle as well?

- ¶ The Major Occultation (939)
- ¶ Death of Percy Bysshe Shelley (1822)
- ¶ Abolition of Catholic Bureau in Germany (1871)
- ¶ William Jennings Bryan's "Cross of Gold" speech (1896)

Thus Endeth LOVE IT OR LEAVE IT WEEK ■

28 WHO'S TO JUDGE WEEK

Wherein is commemorated the fact that burying heads in the soil causes asphyxiation. (1800s)

7/9 WE'RE ALL IN THIS TOGETHER DAY

Christ was meant for all people of all ethnic backgrounds. If each understands Truth, Goodness and Beauty in its own way, then there can be no common science, morality and means of salvation. German Chemistry, French Physics, English Virtue and Italian Genius lie just around the corner!

¶ Gorkum Martyrs (1572)
¶ Birth of Zeger van Espen, Gallican theorist (1646)
¶ Death of Jaime Balmes (1848)

7/10 WHY MUST A NATION BE LIKE A STATE DAY

The Church can exist quite happily simultaneously in different States. A given ethnic group can do the same. A coherent culture is one thing; politics is another. As with every other issue, the primary concern is determining what is just and then pressing States to make just decisions. Ironically, nationalists actually had an ideological political agenda that gave them little in common with the cultures of the peoples whom they claimed to liberate. In reality, they disfigured and exploited them for their anti-national goals.

¶ Catholic League in Germany (1609)
¶ Napoleon dissolves the National Council of Bishops (1811)
¶ Scopes Trial (10–21, 1925)

7/11 BLOW 'EM UP, RUN 'EM DOWN DAY

How were you going to create unified nations in areas where many ethnic groups were mixed? Would minorities have to be deported? Killed? Assimilated? And what about Jews, who seemed to be at home nowhere? Would they have to create their own Nation-State?

¶ Battle of Drogheda (1690)
¶ Birth of Léon Bloy (1846)
¶ Speech of Bishop Vincenz Gasser of Brixen to the Council Fathers in Rome (1870)

7/12 GLOBAL SPRAWL DAY

Since nationalists were really ideologues, enamored of modern English and French models, what they were doing was actually creating one, similar, worldwide "nation"—and a materialist one to boot.

¶ Henry II's penance (1174)
¶ Death of Erasmus (1536)
¶ Civil Constitution of the Clergy (1790)
¶ God sanctions polygamy for the Mormons (1843)
¶ Religious riots in New York (1871)

7/13 DON'T NATIONALIZE, TEMPORIZE DAY

Yes, because of the fact that what really counted to the nationalists was an abstract, non-existent, ideological "homeland," the true, existing nation could be sacrificed by them. Thus, in order to "create Italy," part of Italy, Nice, the home of Garibaldi, was sacrificed by them to France, in exchange for the help of Napoleon III. Help to do what? To build an Italy without the very Italian Niçoise population.

¶ Death of Emperor St. Henry II (1024)
¶ Birth of José Alejo Eyzaguirre, Archbishop elect of Santiago de Chile (1783)

❡ Bathtub murder of Jean-Paul Marat (1793)

❡ Birth of José Manuel Estrada, Argentine Catholic (1842)

❡ Death of Bishop Wilhelm Emmanuel von Ketteler of Mainz (1877)

❡ The Witness of Cardinal Von Galen begins (1941)

7/14 PAY AND MARCH DAY

One of the grand dreams of the unifiers of nations was simply that of ensuring a greater military power for the lands whose cultures they were destroying. This required universal military service, the creation of whole Nations-in-Arms, and, of course, the payment of significantly increased taxes.

❡ St. Edmund Campion arrested (1581)

❡ Birth of Pasquier Quesnel, Jansenist thinker (1634)

❡ Death of Bernard-René de Launy, Governor of the Bastille (1789)

❡ Papal rule restored in Rome (1849)

❡ Death of Bishop Miguel María de la Mora y Mora of San Luis Potosí (1930)

7/15 OH WHAT A HOLY WAR DAY

With one power-hungry nation after another seeking a military place in the sun, war of all against all was only a matter of time. But, given that this type of national aggression was said to be God-willed, perhaps bloody modern warfare was a Divine necessity?

❡ Jerusalem captured (1099)

❡ King Charles II charters the Royal Society (1662)

❡ Signing of French Concordat (1801)

❡ Lifting of *Action Française* ban (1939)

Thus Endeth WHO'S TO JUDGE WEEK ■

29 KINKS IN THE MACHINERY WEEK

Wherein is commemorated the growing willingness to show that blood is thicker than Reason. (1800s)

7/16 ALL IN THE BLOOD DAY

Some mechanists thought that they had found the key to the meaning of life through the study of biology: it was the blood of the specific group to which one belonged that determined everything.
- ¶ Flight of Mohammed from Mecca (622)
- ¶ Beginning of the Great Schism (1054)
- ¶ Anne Askew the Anabaptist burned in England (1546)
- ¶ Fr. Junípero Serra founds Mission in California (1769)
- ¶ Atomic Bomb (1945)

7/17 BLOOD SPORT DAY

The blood of one ethnic group had to be tested against that of the others, since Mother Nature had decreed the struggle of all against all as its most basic laws.
- ¶ Luther enters monastery (1505)
- ¶ Massacre in Champs de Mars (1791)
- ¶ Carmelite Martyrs of Compiegne (1794)
- ¶ Execution of Nicholas II (1918)

7/18 OBVIOUS SELECTION DAY

The best blood will infallibly rise to the top through such a brutal contest, and humanity will progress in consequence. Any loser who does not understand this truth does not understand it precisely because he belongs to an inferior blood group that cannot possibly grasp it. Let the chips fall where they may! Heads will have to roll!

¶ Dogmatic Constitution *Pastor Aeternus* (1870)
¶ Death of Benito Juarez (1872)
¶ Spanish Cruzada Begins (1936)

7/19 ALL THAT WHICH IS EXCELLENT IS OURS DAY

Everything that has ever been of value to human culture is best exemplified in the works of the superior bloodline. All that which is excellent is ours!

¶ Peasants War begins (1524)
¶ Birth of Fr. Ignaz Seipel (1876)
¶ Resignation of Minister Falk of *Kulturkampf* fame (1879)

7/20 MEASURING UP DAY

No one wants his blood group polluted, lest progress be inhibited. Hence, the need to measure skulls, noses, brains, blood types and the like, so that dubious misfits and interlopers can all be discovered and plans for trash collection begin.

¶ Birth of Petrarch (1304)
¶ Napoleon III and Count Cavour concoct unjust war plans at Plombières (1858)
¶ Death of Leo XIII (1903)
¶ Assassination attempt on Hitler (1944)

7/21 AND WE SHALL PURIFY DAY

Legal action would be required once the interlopers were identified. The blood could not be mocked. Culture would triumph. Purity would most certainly be restored. Mother Nature will not be mocked.

¶ Inquisition established (1542)
¶ States of Holland penalize sodomy with death (1730)
¶ *Dominus ac Redemptor* suppressing the Jesuits (1773)

II. ERUPTION SEASON: JULY 85

❡ Kerensky becomes Prime Minister in Russia (1917)
❡ Scopes found guilty (1925)

7/22 ALL THE NATIONS SHALL ADORE THEE DAY

It was not enough simply to be the best. The purified nation with the superior bloodline had to be recognized and worshipped as such by everyone throughout the globe. What fun was being best if no one else openly admitted that you were and grovelled before you?

❡ Godfrey of Bouillon becomes the ruler of Jerusalem (1099)
❡ Death of John Fisher (1535)
❡ Murder of the last Intendant of Paris, Berthier de Sauvigny (1789)

Thus Endeth KINKS IN THE MACHINERY WEEK ■

30 OUT OF THE GAME WEEK

Wherein is commemorated the refusal of those unfit to loosen the laces of the sandals of others to accept the invitation voluntarily to remove themselves. (1800s)

7/23 BLOODY NONSENSE DAY

The Church, from the very outset, could not accept the idea that people must be categorized entirely on the basis of their racial background. The head of the Catholic Centre Party in Germany in the latter nineteenth century even made the point by adopting an African.

❡ Frederick II crowned King of the Romans in Aachen (1215)
❡ The Young Pretender lands in the Hebrides (1745)
❡ Austria-Hungary presents ultimatum to Serbia (1914)

7/24 ALL PAIN, NO GAIN DAY

Towards what end was one progressing by means of all this blood lust struggle? Was the struggle worth the effort? Was it not permissible at least to ask that question?

¶ Death of Matilda, Countess of Tuscany (1115)

¶ Citizens of Leeuwarden, Netherlands, rebel against ban on foreign beer (1487)

¶ Mary, Queen of Scots, forced to abdicate (1567)

7/25 EYE OF THE BEHOLDER DAY

Far from being obvious that any one group was better than another, such estimations were based upon pompous, arbitrary self-flattery, and backed by nothing other than the material strength of the "race" in question. This latest group of preposterous charlatans, as usual, placed truly high culture on a secondary level.

¶ Manifesto of the Duke of Brunswick (1792)

¶ Battle of Custoza (1848)

¶ Murder of Dollfuss (1934)

¶ Seventh Congress of the Comintern proclaiming Popular Front (July 25–August 20, 1935)

¶ *Humanae vitae* (1968)

7/26 DUBIOUS GENETICS DAY

Great minds and cultural achievements have manifestly come from many different ethnic groups. The racists get around this problem by insisting that people have mistakenly attributed the wrong bloodline to geniuses. All that which is excellent becomes indeed theirs! Michelangelo was an Aryan; Plato a Nordic. Dubious genetics triumph across the board.

¶ Francis Pizarro appointed governor of Peru (1529)

¶ Rembrandt declares his insolvency (1656)

II. ERUPTION SEASON: JULY

❧ Birth of Franz Stephan Rautenstrauch, a key Josephist (1734)

❧ Giacomo Casanova arrested in Venice for affronts to religion & common decency (1755)

7/27 STRANGER THAN FICTION DAY

The "scientific" tools used to wean out the unfit earn their right to be worthy of the entire evolutionary vision, filled as it is with dubious missing links and leaps of faith, through their absurd irrationality. Appropriately enough, many of these tools were developed first in California. Nazi legists visited California for enlightenment when preparing the Nüremberg Laws.

❧ Excommunication of Spinoza from the Synagogue (1656)

❧ Robespierre joins the Committee of Public Safety (1793)

❧ Arrest of Robespierre (1794)

❧ The Three Glorious Days (1830)

❧ Birth of Hilaire Belloc (1870)

7/28 BLOODY MESS DAY

What, practically, would one do with the interlopers when identified? Sterilize them so that they do not reproduce? Exile them? Perhaps dispense with them entirely? Purification requires a refiner's fire! But the purifiers would pay an eternal price for their refining work at the hand of a purifying sword of much greater power.

❧ Death of Robespierre (1794)

❧ Birth of Ludwig Feuerbach (1804)

❧ Sentence of Archbishop Primate Antônio de Macedo Costa of Brazil (1874)

❧ Suppression of the *Opera dei Congressi* (1904)

❧ Beginning of World War One (1914)

❧ Death of Albert Houtin, Modernist historian (1926)

7/29 TWO WAY STREET DAY

Nations wishing to display their power on a worldwide level had to build Empires. Empires required roads. Roads could lead the inferior subject peoples into the homelands of their masters. Impurities might actually thus increase rather than diminish. Oh well.

¶ Battle of Kleidan between the Byzantines and the Bulgars (1014)

¶ Unfrocking of Miguel Hidalgo (1811)

¶ *Aeterni Patris* (1868, Convoking Vatican Council)

¶ *Aeterni Patris* (1879, Restoration of Scholastic Philosophy)

¶ Birth of Mussolini (1883)

¶ Murder of Umberto I, King of Italy (1900)

Thus Endeth OUT OF THE GAME WEEK ■

31 REAL CLASS WEEK

Wherein is commemorated the understandable penchant of fraternal equality to develop a mean streak. (1800s)

7/30 NOWHERE TO LAY THEIR HEADS DAY

The mass of people in bourgeois industrial society survives by means of a salary. The masses own nothing, and are therefore part of the proletariat. Democrats and palingenesists claimed to be concerned about this and took copious notes regarding what to do. Trade unions actually did something.

¶ First American Freemasonic Lodge opens in Boston (1733)

¶ First singing of the Marseillaise (1792)

¶ Birth of Werner Jaeger (1888)

¶ Jimmy Hoffa disappears (1975)

7/31 SPONTANEOUS COMBUSTION DAY

The proletariat was said by Marxists to be engaged in inevitable struggle with the bourgeoisie. Class war was a fact of life that could be seen as a key to the machine of nature. My devout proletariat grandparents felt otherwise, but they could easily be eliminated under future, benevolent Marxist leadership.

- Approval of St. Ignatius' Spiritual Exercises (1548)
- Death of Denis Diderot (1784)
- Commission on Church reform in Portugal (1833)
- Austrian Concordat revoked (1870)
- John Ireland becomes Bishop of St. Paul, Minnesota (1884)
- Ley Callas goes into effect in Mexico (1926)

August

8/1 UNBOUNDED LOVE DAY

The problem, as far as anarchists were concerned, was authority, including, especially, the authority of property owners. Get rid of authority of all kinds, and pure love would enable everyone to build the perfect world. Getting to the stage of an anarchist world might involve violence, but such unpleasantness need not take that long. And is not Paradise worth the effort?

¶ Death of Adhemar of Le Puy (1098)
¶ Assassination of Henry III (1589)
¶ Birth of Ludwig von Haller (1768)
¶ Benedict's peace proposals (1917)
¶ Suspension of religious services in Mexico (1926)

8/2 PROFESSORIAL PATIENCE DAY

Marx did not think that unbounded love would solve anything. A proper world would only come about according to a mechanical evolution, which might require centuries for some countries to achieve.

¶ Torquemada made Inquisitor General (1483)
¶ Death of Antoine Arnauld (1694)
¶ Refusal of Fundamental Law for Belgium by Maurice-Jean de Broglie (1815)
¶ Feast of St. Alphonsus Liguori (1696–1787)

II. ERUPTION SEASON: AUGUST

8/3 GUESS WHO'S COMING TO DINNER DAY

Attempts at establishing joint action on behalf of the proletariat brought trade unionists, anarchists and Marxists together in the First International (1864). Its members were not happy campers.

¶ Death of Eugene Sue, anti-Catholic popular novelist (1857)

¶ Hungarian Bolshevik regime collapse (1919)

8/4 MIXED MARRIAGE DAY

Another attempt at union, this time involving a mix of trade unionists and Marxists, created the Second International (1889), with headquarters in Brussels and the exhortation, followed in many countries, to create Social Democratic Parties.

¶ Pope Alexander VIII: *Inter multiplices* vs. Gallicans (1690)

¶ Dom Pérignon invents champagne (1693)

¶ Abolition of Feudalism in France (1789)

8/5 BE TRUE TO YOUR SCHOOL DAY

Different interpretations about what to do with Social Democratic Parties developed. Some "orthodox" Marxists said that they could accomplish nothing other than consciousness-raising among workers, who would have to wait for the historical cycle to move them towards communism, the last stage of development. Others, so-called "Revisionists," said that they needed to be used to effect serious change through the political process. Still others, like Lenin, argued that an elite party that would neither sell-out the Marxist message to vulgar, trade-union demands, nor feel itself condemned passively to await the outcome of history, had to be constructed.

¶ Death of Pio Bruno Lanteri, Founder of the Oblates of the BVM (1830)

¶ Agreement of Chambord and Orleans on the French Succession (1873)

¶ Cornerstone for Statue of Liberty is laid on Bedloe's Island (1884)

Thus Endeth REAL CLASS WEEK ∎

32 MASS MOVING WEEK

Wherein is commemorated the prodding by a thousand stimuli of the same dull mob. (1800s)

8/6 DANGLED TIDBIT DAY

Many people could be tempted to adore capitalism by dangling before them the lucky achievements of a handful of others to spur them on to a live of riches and comfort! Also, people could be won to the support of nefarious capitalist changes because they could not possibly understand their horrible consequences until such time as whole nations and vast numbers were subject to their ravages beyond repair.

¶ Death of Mother Angelique Arnauld (1661)

¶ Parliament bans Jesuits in France (1762)

¶ Birth of Daniel O'Connell (1775)

¶ End of the Holy Roman Empire (1806)

¶ Murder of Garcia Moreno (1875)

¶ Hiroshima (1945)

8/7 SELF-PERPETUATION DAY

Rousseauian ideas about the glorification of the People allowed for individuals to "speak" for everyone else, and thereby perpetuate their own personalities in all those deemed worthy to be called human. Moreover, palingenesis allowed for every new philosophical, political and social force to gain a hearing by calling itself nothing other than the necessary development of absolutely traditional Christian values.

¶ Birth of Baron Franz von Fürstenberg (1729)

¶ *Sollicitudo omnium ecclesiarum* re-establishing the Jesuits (1814)

8/8 FIRM HAND DAY

The idea of a "firm hand," like that of a Bonaparte or another "man on horseback" began to demonstrate its democratic appeal by the last two decades of the nineteenth century. One example was the "Boulangist" movement in France in the 1880s.

¶ Failure of Fifth Crusade in Egypt (1221)

¶ Mary on Throne of England (1553)

¶ Prince Jules Armand de Polignac becomes minister of Charles X (1829)

¶ Execution of Garibaldian priest, Fr. Ugo Bassi (1849)

¶ Death of Ernst Haeckel, Monist (1919)

¶ Death of Don Luigi Sturzo (1959)

8/9 I LOVE A PARADE DAY

Nationalist, militarist themes appealed to the mob as well. The mother of August Bebel, the head of the German Social Democratic Party, was indignant over suggestions by her son's associates that she stop attending parades in Berlin. "I vote for Bebel, but run for the Kaiser," was her response.

¶ Battle of Adrianople (378)

¶ Benito Juarez named Minister of Justice (1855)

¶ Nagasaki (1945)

8/10 THERE GOES THE NEIGHBORHOOD DAY

Racists found the mob an easy target, especially in places like Vienna, which had to deal with immigration problems from all over Austria-Hungary and Russia as well.
- Treaty of Verdun (843)
- Battle of Lechfeld (955)
- Attack on the Tuilleries (1792)
- Alfred Hitchcock's *Psycho* premiered (1960)

8/11 A PENNY FOR YOUR THOUGHTS DAY

The Press became a mass political influence by the latter half of the nineteenth century in countries like England, France and the United States. Here, mass tabloids, costing a pittance, could be used to create war fever and unthinking responses to major national and international issues.
- Death of Johann Tetzel (1519)
- Germany throws out English salesmen (1597)
- Death of John Henry Newman (1890)
- Weimar Constitution (1919)

8/12 OVER THE RAINBOW DAY

Another stimulus to mass movement was the dreams unleashed by migration to America and, in some cases, to the new colonies being obtained by European countries in Africa after the Berlin Congress of 1884–1885.
- Birth of Bishop Pierre Parisis of Langres (1795)
- Death of Pierre Buchez, Christian Socialist (1865)
- Birth of George Soros (1930)
- *Humani generis* (1950)

Thus Endeth MASS MOVING WEEK ■

33 BEATING DEAD HORSES WEEK

Wherein are commemorated the final attempts of a dying civilization to squeeze the last drops of water from already dried-out sponges. (1800s–1900s)

8/13 CULTURAL IMPROVEMENT DAY

Culture Wars—*Kulturkämpfe*—beginning in the Kingdom of Sardinia/Italy, extending into the new German Empire, the French Third Republic and, for a time, in Austria-Hungary and the Lowlands as well, were unleashed as a means of getting rid of the last Christian "idols" standing in the way of Progress.

¶ Titus Oates Plot (1678)
¶ Birth of Archbishop Michael Augustine Corrigan of New York (1839)

8/14 CHILDREN'S SAFARI DAY

The latter part of the nineteenth century witnessed a variety of countries establish mandatory educational systems in which students were deprived of religious training and even raised in an anti-Christian spirit. Reaction on the part of Catholic parents in places like the Lowlands was ferocious.

¶ Death of Pius II (1464)
¶ Jesuits welcomed back to Austria (1820)
¶ Polish defeat of Reds (1920)
¶ Atlantic Charter (1941)

8/15 EMPTYING THE CONVENTS DAY

Similarly, new assaults on religious orders and congregations, especially those that were involved in education, were pressed to the utmost.

¶ St. Ignatius at Montmartre (1534)
¶ Birth of Napoleon (1769)
¶ *Mirari vos* (1832)
¶ Formation of the Italian National Society (1857)

8/16 SEPARATION DAY

Separation of Church and State was always a major concern of revolutionary governments, from those that were liberal to the most radical. Pursued with renewed fervor in this age, the most important separation that took place was that in France in 1903.
¶ Death of Bishop Ignaz von Senestry of Regensburg (1906)
¶ Death of John Courtney Murray (1967)

8/17 CLOAK AND DAGGER DAY

Many groups became ever more engaged in secret organization, terrorism, counterterrorism and acts of civil disobedience as the era drew to a close. "It will come, it will come," some anarchists sang; "every bourgeois will have his bomb." Fanatical national societies were not the least of such perilous political participants.
¶ Death of King Frederick II of Prussia (1786)
¶ Charles Darwin leaves South America (1836)
¶ Götterdämmerung premieres in Bayreuth (1876)
¶ *Animal Farm* is published (1946)

8/18 SOLIDARITY DAY

Enthusiasts for global solidarity and eternal peace could be found in ever increasing numbers by the turn of the century. Andrew Carnegie was one of them; various Social Democrats were others. Unfortunately, the philosophies underlying the different expressions of hope for peace were ones that insisted upon the omnipresence of struggle in nature and human life, or gave no ground for being able to identify, objectively, anything that was right or wrong. Why bother?

¶ Death of Genghis Khan (1227)

¶ French Concordat (1516)

¶ Austrian Concordat (1855)

8/19 PRISONERS OF WAR DAY

Propaganda for war as a purifying, progressive force became ever more strident by the turn of the new century as well. Futurists even saw it as a source of artistic beauty, some of them arguing that bodies twisted by shrapnel or barbed wire were objects of particular splendor.

¶ Aenea Silvio Piccolomini becomes Pope Pius II (1458)

¶ Nicholas II installs the Imperial Duma (1905)

¶ Mohammed Mosaddegh overturned by the Americans and the British in Iran (1953)

Thus Endeth BEATING DEAD HORSES WEEK ∎

34 FINGERS IN THE DIKE WEEK

Wherein is commemorated Catholic opening of umbrellas during Monsoon Season. (1800s–1900s)

8/20 INTO THE TOWER DAY

Civilization is dying all around us, some Catholics argued. The only way to deal with our problems is to hide within the confines of the parish and Church organizations and let the curtain come down on the whole corrupt structure.

¶ Death of St. Bernard (1153)

¶ Speech of Montalembert on Church and State at Malines (1863)

¶ Death of Pius X (1914)

8/21 OUT OF THE TOWER DAY

Nonsense, others responded. The structure itself is morally indifferent. Catholics must play an open role within it and thereby compel it down an acceptable direction.

¶ Death of Peter Lombard (1160)
¶ Buda captured by the Turks (1524)
¶ Birth of Jules Michelet (1798)

8/22 HOPELESS ADMONITION DAY

Some Catholics who were convinced that civilization was collapsing, but who nevertheless wished to try to do something to save it, wanted the Papacy to give instruction to believers regarding the rights and wrongs of contemporary society. The first fruit of this enterprise was the publication by Pius IX of the *Syllabus of Errors* (1864), a list of eighty principles of modernity which Catholics could never accept.

¶ St. Columba reports seeing monster in Loch Ness (565)
¶ Battle of Bosworth Field (1485)
¶ Birth of Pierre Cardinal de Tencin (1680)

8/23 SOCIAL DOCTRINE DAY

The *Syllabus of Errors* focused on the mistakes of the Enlightenment and the Revolution. But was there a positive, Catholic teaching that could serve as a guide for dealing with current political and social problems? Leo XIII (1878–1903) began the process of formulating just such a substantive Catholic Social Doctrine.

¶ Pope Paul III's Reform Commission (1536)
¶ Proclamation of the *Levée en Masse* (1793)
¶ Austria excluded from the German Confederation (1866)
¶ Hitler-Stalin Pact (1939)

8/24 WILD PARTY DAY

The presumption of those who wished to come out of the tower was that Catholic political parties should be formed to contest elections, which were indeed becoming ever more democratic. These parties could run into major problems over specific policies beyond the purely defensive ones of standing guard over the rights of the Church. The Catholic Centre Party in Germany is a good example.

- ⁋ St. Bartholomew's Day Massacre begins (1572)
- ⁋ Birth of Bartolomé Herrara, Peruvian Catholic (1808)
- ⁋ Liberal Revolution in Portugal (1820)
- ⁋ Death of Comte de Chambord (1883)

8/25 KING AND COUNTRY DAY

Legitimism was reinvigorated as a political movement, emphasizing its pro-Catholic characteristics in the work of men such as Charles Maurras and his *Action Française*. "Politics first!" was its motto, indicating its conviction that the salvation of religion was dependent upon the reestablishment of a traditional monarchy dedicated to the maintenance of the French nation and all that made it great.

- ⁋ Death of David Hume (1776)
- ⁋ Capture of rebellious Marseilles by Republicans (1793)
- ⁋ Belgian Revolution (1830)
- ⁋ Death of Friedrich Nietzsche (1900)
- ⁋ *Notre Charge Apostolique* condemns the Sillon (1910)

8/26 WRONG SIDE OF THE TRACKS DAY

Some Catholics were horrified by liberal capitalist flouting of economic morality and indifference to all social consequences of individual greed. Others were outraged by socialist assaults on individual property ownership. If political activism there had to be, each said, then let it take place in union with others who thought similarly, regardless of their religious affiliations. Alas, each group

considered the other to be on the wrong side of the tracks.
- ⁋ Refractory clergy ordered out of France (1792)
- ⁋ Birth of Mother Teresa (1910)
- ⁋ Foundation of World Council of Churches (1948)

Thus Endeth FINGERS IN THE DIKE WEEK ∎

35 ANYTHING GOES WEEK

Wherein are commemorated the currents mindlessly taking all refuse to the sea. (1890s–1914)

8/27 BOUNDLESS OPTIMISM DAY

Many people, fed by Social Darwinism, Marxism, continued Liberal beliefs and insipid popular Enlightenment writers, were as pleased as punch with their era, and could see nothing but hope for the future in it. *Gaudium et Spes* before its time!
- ⁋ Birth of Georg Wilhelm Friedrich Hegel (1770)
- ⁋ Declaration of the Rights of Man (1789)
- ⁋ Declaration of Pilnitz (1791)

8/28 HOPELESS PESSIMISM DAY

Many others, aware of the endless divisions of thought in the modern world and the fanatical commitment of the various proponents of this myriad of positions, became convinced that they lived in the worst of eras, and one that was headed towards an inevitable cataclysm. *O tempora, o mores!*
- ⁋ Death of St. Augustine (430)
- ⁋ Pope Paul V's prohibition of further disputes on Grace (1607)
- ⁋ Birth of Amalie von Gallitzyn (1748)
- ⁋ *Auctorem fidei* vs. the Synod of Pistoia (1794)
- ⁋ Birth of Jaime Balmes (1810)

8/29 LURID PASSION DAY

All that matters is the individual, some cried. Indulge those passions—the more base, the better! What glory there was in the decadence pervading much of turn of the century culture!

- Battle of Mohacs (1526)
- Death of Ulrich von Hutten (1523)
- Birth of John Locke (1632)
- Death of Pius VI (1799)

8/30 ATONAL DAY

With no rules left to guide life, the arts were free to go stark raving mad as well. Why should there be any guidelines for colors, shapes, keys, word definitions or anything else? Atonal music for an atonal world!

- Anne Hutchinson condemned (1637)
- Birth of Fr. Emmanuel d'Alzon, Founder of the Assumptionists (1810)
- Religious instruction compulsory in Belgian State Schools (1895)
- Attempt on Lenin's life (1918)

8/31 SONG OF THE DEED DAY

Anarchists were convinced that a few simple "deeds" of a new type of knight errant could ring out the old and bring in the new. These deeds could be assassinations; they could also be the unleashing of General Strikes. Bayonne, New Jersey was a hotbed of anarchist strategic planning. Can anything good actually come out of Bayonne, New Jersey???

- Beginning of Directory attacks on religion in Belgium (1796)
- Pope approves renewed Benedictines in France (1837)
- Birth of Georg von Hertling, Catholic activist (1843)
- Death of Charles Baudelaire (1867)

September

9/1 WELCOMING ARMAGEDDON DAY

Nihilists believed that nothing had any meaning. The great benefit of the twentieth century—which, as Nietzsche described it, would be a century of war, revolution, disease, famine and massive inhumanity—was that it would demonstrate this meaninglessness infallibly to everyone.

¶ King Louis XIV dies (1715)
¶ Foundation of the National Prohibition Party (1869)
¶ *Sacrorum antistitum* and the Oath against Modernism (1910)

9/2 DESTROYING WHAT OTHER MEN CHERISH DAY

Would some people be horrified by the coming twentieth century Armageddon? Of course! This was due to the fact that they did not want to get rid of the security blanket of ideas that convinced them that there was some truth and goodness guiding life. No matter! The only real good was the revelation of meaninglessness; the destruction of what other men cherished.

¶ The Great Fire of London (1666)
¶ Death of Bishop Nicholas von Hontheim, Founder of Febronianism (1790)
¶ Revolutionary Prison massacres in Paris (2–6, 1792)

Thus Endeth ANYTHING GOES WEEK ■

36 WHERE IS THIS GOING WEEK

Wherein is commemorated the reality that Enlightenment and Progress were dropping dead like flies. (1914)

9/3 WHAT'S THE POINT AND WHERE'S THE JOY DAY

Optimism was not hope; it was not built upon anything more solid than sentimental desire. The Enlightenment thinker seeing nothing but building blocks to a better future coming from his vision of life was only examining half of the evidence.
- ¶ French Invasion of Italy (1494)
- ¶ Death of Oliver Cromwell (1658)
- ¶ Condemnation of the *Encyclopedia* (1759)
- ¶ French Constitution (1791)

9/4 WHAT ELSE DID YOU EXPECT DAY

Of course the reduction of life to nothing but nature had to unleash all of the endless conflicting desires of the lower side of man's character: all the divisions and passion for destructive struggle that had been predicted by the Church since the beginning of the modern era.
- ¶ Coup of 18 Fructidor vs. the Regalists (1797)
- ¶ Birth of Fr. Carlo Maria Curci, S.J. (1810)
- ¶ Opium War begins (1839)
- ¶ Death of Charles Peguy (1914)

9/5 RITES OF SPRING/REALITY OF SUMMER DAY

The unleashing of passion was now bearing its fruit in the mindless descent into war by August of 1914, when the sister nations of Europe decided to destroy one another for no good reason whatsoever.

¶ Terror as the "Order of the Day" decreed (1793)
¶ *Chambre introuvable* dissolved (1816)
¶ William George Ward received in Church (1845)

9/6 MUD DAY

The idea of a quick, glorious, purifying war quickly degenerated into a dreadful trench conflict, alternating mass boredom and mass butchery under daily living conditions of subhuman character.

¶ Battle of Nördlingen (1634)
¶ Austrians occupy Belgrade (1688)
¶ Consecration of Bishop Michael Heiss at Green Bay (1868)
¶ William McKinley shot (1901)

9/7 MANPOWER DAY

The veneer of civility still remaining over the fetid lusts of the Enlightenment was swiftly pulled away by the war. A decline of the language reflected the growing indifference to life and the dignity of man. Hence, as the Austrian critic Karl Kraus noted, the willingness to refer to "manpower" needs as one had once made reference to "horsepower."

¶ The assault on Boniface VIII at Anagni (1303)
¶ Birth of Thomas Erastus (1524)

9/8 PAPAL TREASON DAY

Benedict XV (1914–1922) had the temerity to express the conviction that everyone was at fault in this conflict, and that governments should be satisfied with the damage that they had already done. Men on both sides of the trenches could consider him wanting for not recognizing the obvious moral superiority of their cause.

II. ERUPTION SEASON: SEPTEMBER

⁋ Encyclical *Unigenitus* (1713)
⁋ Excommunication of the Jansenist Appellants (1718)
⁋ Pius X's attack on Modernism: *Pascendi* (1907)

9/9 WAR TO END ALL WARS DAY

Woodrow Wilson could not endure the Papal suggestion that the war end by means of negotiation conducted by the representatives of both of the guilty alliance systems. The Entente Powers were the Good combating Evil Personified. A fight until victory would ensure that this would be a War to End All Wars.

⁋ Conference at Poissy begins (1561)
⁋ Louis XV vs. the French *parlements* (1730)
⁋ Madame Pompadour meets Louis XV (1745)

Thus Endeth WHERE IS THIS GOING WEEK *and, with it,* ERUPTION SEASON ■

III. CONSEQUENCE SEASON:
"Nothing to kill or die for"
(1900S ONWARDS)

37 TRIUMPH OF THE WILL WEEK

Wherein are commemorated the all too impressive imprints left by a few persons' choices on most persons' lives. (1900s)

9/10 MAGIC MOUNTAIN DAY

Thomas Mann's novel, *The Magic Mountain*, presents for us a sick western world, paralyzed by the clash of its manifold contestants for an intellectual hearing, and now reduced to a perpetual, ineffective debating society. Mynheer Peeperkorn, a man of mindless will and strength, shows how easily these paper tigers can be bent to follow his powerful but irrational commands.

¶ Pius IX proclaims the *Non expedit* policy in Italy (1874)
¶ Murder of the Empress Elizabeth (1898)

9/11 ELAN VITAL DAY

Many thinkers approved of the need to rely on the guidance of the willful and the strong. Any manifestation of such vitality was a revelation of life, the truth that brings life to full vigor, and the nature of whatever "god" stands behinds this energy. The thrust of vital spirit was irresistible. Henri Bergson was one of the most important promoters of this argument, whether he wanted to be so or not.

III. CONSEQUENCE SEASON: SEPTEMBER 107

- ¶ Abbey of Cluny founded (910)
- ¶ Massacre of Drogheda (1649)
- ¶ Invasion of Papal States (1860)

9/12 TAKE MY LEAD DAY

Observation of front line soldiers during the First World War demonstrated the possibility of uniting the endlessly varied factions of modern life in obedience to officers in the trenches. Benito Mussolini (1883–1945) deduced from this the argument that transposing the "leadership principle" from the crisis of the front to the crisis of daily civilian life might be equally effective.

- ¶ Swiss centralization measures (1848)
- ¶ Birth of H.L. Mencken (1880)
- ¶ Birth of John Courtney Murray (1904)
- ¶ Gabriele D'Annunzio's attack on Fiume (1919)

9/13 BUDDIES EACH AND EVERY ONE DAY

One of the most appealing features of life on the front for a man like Mussolini was the fact that it made comrades of everyone in the trenches, regardless of their class background. Again, perhaps the answer to endemic class strife was the introduction of the frontline experience into the life of the divided population behind the lines as well.

- ¶ Battle of Marignano (1515)
- ¶ Return of Calvin to Geneva (1541)
- ¶ Death of Montaigne (1592)
- ¶ Death of Philip II (1598)
- ¶ Fall of Quebec (1759)
- ¶ Death of Ludwig Feuerbach (1872)
- ¶ Leo XIII's *Apostolicae curae* (1896)

9/14 ME NE FREGO DAY

Mussolini formed his bands (*fasci di combattimento*) of "peacetime" front-line soldiers in Milan in 1919, outfitting them in black shirts evocative of anarchist symbolism. Their only overriding command was to obey the leader, the *duce*. If asked what, specifically, they were proposing to cure Italy's ills, their response was "I don't give a damn" (*me ne frego*) thereby indicating that the answer would only emerge out of the vital will of the leader and action for action's sake: not from any pre-conceived ideas.

¶ The Great Fire of Moscow begins (1812)
¶ First volume of *Das Kapital* (1867)
¶ Grand Orient eliminates need for belief in God (1877)
¶ Peter Stolypin murdered (1911)
¶ Miguel Primo de Rivera becomes dictator in Spain (1923)

9/15 WHO WANTS THEM ANYWAY DAY (A.K.A. MARGARET SANGER DAY)

Mussolini had many imitators, one of them, Adolf Hitler (1889–1945), adding racial theory to the leadership principle. Anyone who accepted him as leader would have to agree to the need for the leading race to protect itself and guide the world.

¶ Birth of Joseph Hergenröther, Church historian (1824)
¶ Removal of John Joseph Keane as Rector of Catholic University (1896)
¶ Nüremberg Laws (1935)

9/16 FEEL THOSE MUSCLES DAY

Some religious minded thinkers, concerned for the question of how, more effectively, to evangelize the world, both outside and inside Europe, began to espouse the theory of the need to merge with the successful vital energies that they encountered around them. Only by

thus abandoning oneself to "vigor" could a narrow, "loser" individualist become a truly "triumphant person."
- ⁋ John II Casimir abdicates to become a Jesuit (1668)
- ⁋ Napoleonic Italian Concordat (1803)
- ⁋ Martyrdom of Fr. Amadio Bertoncelli (1809)
- ⁋ Grito de Dolores in Mexico (1810)
- ⁋ Wall Street bombing (1920)

Thus Endeth TRIUMPH OF THE WILL WEEK ∎

38 WHERE THERE'S A WILL THERE'S A BILL WEEK

Wherein is commemorated the Catholic desire to demur at the honor of being chosen to obey bestowed upon them by strongly-willed acquaintances. (1900s)

9/17 EASE OFF AND KEEP YOUR DISTANCE DAY

Strong, willful personalities can be nothing other than an irritating and permanent pain in the neck. Catholics prefer every protection against their mindless predatory behavior that is possible.
- ⁋ Battle of Myriocephalon (1176)
- ⁋ Absolution of Henry IV (1595)
- ⁋ Law of Suspects in France (1793)
- ⁋ Birth of Heinrich Pesch, a Father of Catholic Economics (1854)
- ⁋ Revolution in Spain (1868)

9/18 COLD SHOWER DAY

Orthodox Catholic teaching takes it for granted that one has to lose his soul in Christ in order to gain it more fully. Looking to one's own will for guidance is a recipe for collapsing into a meaningless abyss. Modernity requires a bath in self-denial.

❡ Birth of Johann Heinrich Cardinal Frankenberg, Archbishop of Mâlines (1726)

❡ Synod of Pistoia (18–28, 1786)

❡ Battle of Castelfidardo (1860)

9/19 STOP, LOOK AND LISTEN DAY

War is not man's normal condition, and it ought not to be the case that people blindly follow the equivalent of a field officer in ordinary civil life.

❡ The first hot air balloon ascends at Versailles (1783)

❡ Siege of Paris begins (1870)

9/20 A TABLE FOR ONE DAY

Constant communal activity, without any space for individual meditation and action, can, in the long run, be just as soul-killing as liberal atomism.

❡ Election of Robert of Geneva as "Clement VII" (1378)

❡ Battle of Valmy (1792)

❡ Carlsbad Decrees (1819)

❡ Death of Fr. Luigi Taparelli d'Azeglio—some sources say 21st (1862)

❡ Italian Robbery of Papal Rome (1870)

9/21 DEFINITION DAY

Aristotelian logic does not disappear, simply because many people disagree with one another. The principle of non-contradiction is not abolished due to the imposition of the will of the more powerful. You, personally, may not give a damn about "things," but those "things" will come back to give you hell for neglecting them.

❡ Burning of Fr. Gabriel Malagrida, SJ, in Lisbon (1761)

❡ Proclamation of French Republic and beginning of Year One (1792)

❡ Death of Arthur Schopenhauer (1860)

❡ Birth of H.G. Wells (1866)

III. CONSEQUENCE SEASON: SEPTEMBER

9/22 SITTING DUCKS AT LOURDES DAY

Everyone is endangered, theoretically, when the leadership principle is the sole guide for civil society. In practice, security depends here solely on the personality of the leader. Mussolini was somewhat gentle; Hitler, not at all. Since the racially impure were considered to be sick elements in the body politic, they were a bit like pilgrims at a sacred healing site, the difference being that the ill went to the shrine for a cure and the *Untermenschen* lined up to be shot.

¶ Birth of Gaspar Cardinal Mermillod, Bishop and Catholic Social Activist (1824)

¶ Otto von Bismarck becomes Prussian Prime Minister (1862)

9/23 LEFT OVER LAMENNAIS DAY

"Personalists," as a number of religious opponents of liberal individualism called themselves, were in many respects merely resurrecting Lamennais' ideas, along with his grant of power to determine what was or was not a legitimate "energy" to charismatic prophets. But then again, the actual meaning of Personalism will only be revealed on Judgment Day.

¶ Concordat of Worms (1122)

¶ Birth of Jaques Crétineau-Joly, Catholic apologist (1803)

¶ First Organic Law on education in Belgium (1842)

¶ Death of Sigmund Freud (1939)

Thus Endeth WHERE THERE'S A WILL THERE'S A BILL WEEK ■

39 DIZZY WITH SUCCESS WEEK

Wherein is commemorated the hangover left by exaggerated love for political parties. (1900s)

9/24 PUPPET DAY

Lenin wanted to give all power to the Soviets because he realized that his Bolsheviks could easily control them. He had no interest in giving power to these councils in and of themselves.
- ¶ Liberius ends his reign as Pope (366)
- ¶ Death of Pippin (768)
- ¶ Mormons renounce polygamy (1890)

9/25 THE PARTY'S OVER DAY

The party as Lenin conceived it required a tight administration to function properly. A General Secretary was needed to keep the structure under control. Unfortunately, the Party, under Joseph Stalin, ended by being nothing other than an instrument of its Secretary.
- ¶ Peace of Augsburg (1555)
- ¶ Benedict Arnold joins the British (1780)

9/26 MACHINE MAN DAY

The Party controlled by Stalin was a mindless machine demanding the labors of mindless minions subservient to the will the General Secretary—apparatchiks.
- ¶ Birth of Bishop Louis-Édouard Cardinal Pie of Poitiers (1815)
- ¶ Birth of Holy Alliance (1815)
- ¶ Condemnation of Georg Hermes (1835)
- ¶ Birth of T.S. Eliot (1888)
- ¶ Birth of Martin Heidegger (1889)
- ¶ Suppression of the Leonine Prayers (1964)

9/27 WHO NEEDS TO EAT DAY

Collectivization from 1929 onwards involved an enormous amount of suffering on the part of the entire Soviet population. It also led to the first man-made famine in world history, and the death of some millions of people, Ukrainians at the head of the list.

¶ Regimini militantes ecclesiae confirming the Society of Jesus (1540)

¶ Charles X makes his state entry into Paris (1824)

9/28 SPRING CLEANING DAY

Some Party members could not convincingly play the role of apparatchiks. Others could, but remembered the days before Stalin came to full power with unacceptable nostalgia. Others were simply *personae non gratae* for any reason at all. Time to open the windows and toss these corpses on the rubbish heap of history to the winds!

¶ Pompey the Great assassinated (48 B.C.)

¶ Antipope Benedict XIII elected (1394)

¶ Napoleon graduates from the École Militaire in Paris (1785)

¶ Mass for Louis XVI in the Quirinale (1793)

¶ Leo XII elected Pope (1823)

9/29 HEGELIAN FLIP-FLOP DAY

Marx, following Hegel, believed that history evolved. What was true yesterday might not be true today. In Soviet Russia, the General Secretary—a.k.a. the Party and a.k.a. the interpreter of history—knew when it was time for yet another evolution. Enemies today, friends tomorrow!

¶ Frederick II excommunicated (1227)

¶ Birth of Comte de Chambord (1820)

¶ Death of Émile Zola (1902)

9/30 LOVE IS BLIND DAY

Some western anti-fascists wanted to believe that life was glorious in the Soviet Union. Hard as they looked amidst the dead and dying bodies, everything, as far as they were concerned, was coming up roses. Was this a sign of the new Marxist-Leninist aesthetics?

¶ Remonstrant Society formed in Amsterdam (1619)

¶ Otto von Bismarck delivers his "Blood and Iron" speech (1862)

¶ Queen Isabella II of Spain flees the country (1868)

Thus Endeth DIZZY WITH SUCCESS WEEK ∎

October

40 RUN FOR YOUR LIFE WEEK

Wherein are commemorated the checking of excess members of the Christian population and the provision of plenty of fresh, cold air to enjoy to many, many others. (1900s)

10/1 THE EAST IS DEAD DAY

The ecclesiastical hierarchy and the monastic culture of Russian Orthodoxy were devastated by the Soviets in the course of the 1920s and early 1930s. No new Patriarch could be chosen after the death of Nikon in 1924. Seminaries, monasteries and most churches were closed, many of the most venerable torn down or devoted to other purposes, including service as prisons. The Society of the Godless directed propaganda and often deadly violent action versus the Orthodox. But Latin Christians and Protestants also suffered under this Reign of Terror.

¶ Birth of Othmar Spann, Catholic philosopher, sociologist, and economist (1878)
¶ First Five Year Plan (1928)
¶ Franco proclaimed Head of State (1936)

10/2 MEXICAN PEASANT DAY

The Mexican revolutionary government took a radically anti-Catholic turn in the 1920s as Masonic and then Marxist elements became more and more daring in their attacks. The Church fought back by prohibiting all services—which could only be held under unacceptable government conditions—in 1926. The armed resistance of Catholic peasants, the *Cristeros*, took the government by surprise, its fury and success only being undercut by the betrayal of the *Arreglos* of 1929.

¶ Birth of Fr. Augustin de Barruel, S.J. (1741)

¶ Death of Sam Adams (1803)

¶ End of Warsaw uprising (1944)

¶ Dissenters publish protest against *Humanae Vitae* in the New York Times (1968)

10/3 PEACE AND BROTHERHOOD DAY

Soviet foreign policy was resolutely opposed to cooperation with other political forces before 1933. After 1933, fear of Hitler gradually caused the Comintern to promote Popular Front movements, seeking to unite all anti-fascist groups in a fraternal effort to maintain the Versailles settlement. Many feared that these "front movements" were solely designed to promote Soviet interests.

¶ Saladin takes Jerusalem (1187)

¶ Edgar Allen Poe found delirious in a gutter in Baltimore (1849)

¶ Venice given to Italy (1866)

10/4 RAIN IN SPAIN DAY

Spain was one country where a Popular Front movement took power, in early 1936. This immediately proceeded down an often violent anti-Catholic direction, culminating in the murder of the Catholic party leader, Calvo Sotelo, and occasioning the uprising of the Generals in July of the same year. The Republic gradually came to be dominated by the small Communist segment of the Loyalist population in its conflict with the Nationalists.

❡ Birth of Archbishop Peter Pázmány of Esztergom (1570)
❡ Napoleon quells Royalists at St. Roche (1795)
❡ Birth of Engelbert Dollfuss (1892)

10/5 NO MATTER WHICH WAY YOU TURN DAY

The alliance of the Soviets with the Anglo-Americans in the Second World War proved to be a disastrous dilemma for the Catholics. Most would have been happy to see the Nazis defeated by the latter; the idea that this would lead also to the victory of the former made it seem as though all the consequences of the conflict were intolerable.

❡ Women's March on Versailles (1789)
❡ Portuguese Republic (1910)
❡ Locarno Conference (1925)

10/6 USEFUL PRELATE DAY

Stalin changed policy towards the Russian Church in 1941, seeing in it a useful ally versus Germany. Orthodox prelates continued to be willing spokesmen for the foreign policy goals of the regime even when its friendliness disappeared under Khrushchev. East Bloc countries, after the war, also witnessed the attempt by Marxist governments to involve so-called "Pax Priests" in the struggle for tranquility and equality against the warmongering and grasping policies of the capitalist nations.

❡ Louis XVI returns to Paris from Versailles (1789)
❡ Nabisco Foods invents Cream of Wheat (1893)
❡ Death of Albert de Mun (1914)

10/7 LIBERATION DAY

Worker priests, clerics in labor and concentration camps and Personalists galore all began to argue by the 1940s that Catholics could only "win" by abandoning themselves to the "energy" released by the pro-Marxist masses seeking liberation from capitalist exploitation. Once again, charismatic prophets of Marxist orientation were said to be needed to stimulate this energy, ultimately through training for liberation in base communities. South America became a center for such activity, but often at the hands of European activists who were first aroused by the "energy" that they felt was unleashed by the National Revolution in the early years of Vichy France.

¶ Battle of Lepanto (1571)
¶ Death of Giuseppe Toniolo (1918)

Thus Endeth RUN FOR YOUR LIFE WEEK ∎

41 FROM BURGHER TO BURGER WEEK

Wherein is commemorated the French-frying of the medieval city. (late 1800s–present)

10/8 MAN WITHOUT A COUNTRY DAY

International Capitalism grew in the course of the nineteenth and twentieth centuries, convincing not only nationalists, but ordinary patriots as well, that it had no particular commitments to any given land. Its homeland was wherever profit could be gained. Nationalists and ordinary patriots realized that they should act accordingly.

¶ Council of Chalcedon begins (451)
¶ Birth of Archbishop Hyacinthe Louis de Quélen of Paris (1778)
¶ Hitler Youth storm Archbishop's palace in Vienna (1938)

10/9 NOTHING TO DO WITH THE MARKET DAY

Profits more and more seem to have nothing to do with production. Markets go down when employment is high; they go up before a commodity even exists. Moreover, after 1960, the things that are produced seem to have little to do with any discernable basic human need.

⁋ John Henry Newman becomes a Catholic (1845)
⁋ Rome made capital of the Kingdom of Italy (1870)
⁋ Birth of Jackson de Figueredo, Founder of Centro Dom Vital (1891)
⁋ Death of Pius XII (1958)

10/10 MATURE DEBTOR DAY

In the nineteenth century, Balzac took for granted the bad consequences of debt upon a man's reputation. In the second half of the twentieth century, flipping around to respond to the latest demand of the elitist driven *Zeitgeist*, he would be forced to catalogue the evil effects on a person's reputation of failure to owe enough money. Woe to the solvent!

⁋ Battle of Tours (732)
⁋ Imperial-Papal battle at Diet of Würzburg (1157)
⁋ Birth of Fr. Antonio Ballerini, SJ, writer for *La Civiltà Cattolica* (1805)

10/11 POINTLESS CHANGE AND USELESS MOTION DAY

As global capitalism requires more and more tricks to survive, it is forced to encourage a constant changing of every fashion and of every consumer good. Failure to sell and to convince people to toss their previous purchases into the gutter becomes the equivalent of death. Nevertheless, in reality, there grows less and less reason to change anything or go anywhere, since all things are ever more similar.

℘ Death of Ulrich Zwingli (1531)
℘ Birth of François Mauriac (1885)
℘ Opening of Second Vatican Council (1962)

10/12 IMPORTUNING TOURIST DAY

Tourism is an important source of moneymaking for some of the machine parts of the growing Global Motherland. Tourists, however, are confused and offended by many of the unfamiliar practices of the lands that they visit. But they also dislike the local population's failure to perform upon demand quaint dances that travel agencies have invented and claimed to be beloved by the People at large. Pointless change and the creation of new and artificial "traditions" to satisfy the market are here too *de rigeur*.

℘ Cyrus the Great takes Babylon (539 B.C.)
℘ Honorius ends his Papacy (638)
℘ America's first asylum opens for 'Persons of Insane and Disordered Minds' in Virginia (1773) — Test case for the entire population (according to Ezra Pound)
℘ Birth of Christopher Dawson (1889)
℘ Death of Anatole France (1924)

10/13 MOVEABLE FEAST DAY

Holidays are good for shopping, but bad for business if they disrupt the workweek. Why not move all holidays to Mondays, so as to increase the shopping potential of the weekend with the least damage to productive labor? Who cares if they signify anything any more?

℘ Arrest of the Templars (1307)
℘ Emperor Joseph II's Patent of Toleration (1781)
℘ Miracle of the Sun (1917)
℘ Conciliar Coup d'état of Cardinal Liénart and his allies (1962)

10/14 GLOBAL SHOPPING DAY

Why should one be forced to strain the mind to understand the difference of goods sold in lands visited on holiday? Why shouldn't goods that one appreciates be sold everywhere at every moment? To hell with distinction! It interferes with immediate gratification. Better to buy foreign souvenirs around the corner from the apartment and familiar goods in Ouagadougou.

¶ Battle of Hastings (1066)
¶ Trial of Mary, Queen of Scots (1586)
¶ A.A. Milne's *Winnie the Pooh* (1926)

Thus Endeth FROM BURGHER TO BURGER WEEK ■

42 SAVE THE NEIGHBORHOOD WEEK

Wherein is commemorated the shameless effort of disreputable Rednecks to avoid suicide. (1700s onwards)

10/15 WHISTLING DIXIE DAY

Louis XVI's Minister of War already noted in June of 1789 that everything had been sold out, lock, stock and barrel to the interests of the capitalists. It was not that he thought that the moneymen should have no say in life; simply that they should not have the sole control of it. One of the values that should have some continued influence is patriotic devotion to the land of one's birth or voluntary choice—even if a man might make more money by betraying the Fatherland.

¶ Birth of Friedrich Nietzsche (1844)
¶ Arrest of Alfred Dreyfus (1894)

10/16 BRING YOUR OWN BOTTLE DAY

In a market that bears no relation to reality, flourishing *trattorie* that everyone can afford are replaced by restaurants that are the sole preserve of the wealthy—who then swiftly abandon them and the quarters in which they are located for flippant, though terribly destructive, reasons. Ah, for the days when one could bring his own bottle to the local dive! Or, at least, pay a price for it bearing some relation to its true cost!

¶ Feast of St. Margaret Mary Alacoque (1647–1690)

¶ Protests erupt over Joseph II's secularizing reforms in Belgium (1786)

¶ Execution of Marie Antoinette (1793)

¶ The Battle of the Nations (1813)

¶ *L'Avenir* (1830)

¶ The Long March of the Chinese Communists (1934)

10/17 EBENEZER SCROOGE DAY

No self-respecting nineteenth century banker would lend money to people who were continuously in debt. In fact, no self-respecting person would lend a dime to a friend similarly cursed. Holding on to what one has actually got in his pocket until being certain of the ability to pay for what he desires to purchase might not be a bad principle after all.

¶ Birth of Saint Simon (1760)

¶ Defeat of the Vendée at Cholet (1793)

¶ Battle of Campo Formio (1797)

¶ Birth of Cardinal Franz Ehrle, S.J. (1845)

10/18 PARTICIPATORY DEMOCRACY DAY

But why should the neighbourhood change, against the will of those who live there? If democracy has any significance and value anywhere, surely it ought to be on the local level. Why should the block be busted solely because Change wants to move in?

¶ Revocation of Edict of Nantes (1685)

¶ German Democratic Republic leader Erich Honecker resigns (1989)

III. CONSEQUENCE SEASON: OCTOBER

10/19 DON'T ARCH YOUR BACK FOR THE VISITORS DAY

The whole rhythm of a culture, including what it eats and drinks, how it celebrates, when it conducts its festivals, and what it is that these celebrations include ought not to be solely determined by the tourist profit motive. If it is, it will thereby become fraudulent and ultimately die.

¶ Birth of Marsilio Ficino (1433)
¶ Napoleon begins his retreat from Moscow (1812)
¶ Death of Plutarco Calles (1945)

10/20 DEEP FREEZE AND PARALYSIS DAY

Events and individuals have a meaning. To strip them from their context is deadly to their "fresh" nature, true character and the quality of life in general. It withers them, strips them of their real "flavor," and deprives them of their ability to fuel the *élan vital* of a vibrant culture.

¶ Maria Theresa gains power in Austria (1740)
¶ Arrest of Archbishop Graf Cardinal von Franckenberg of Mâlines (1797)
¶ Birth of Bill Gates, eugenicist, vaccine maniac and general nuisance (1955)

10/21 LOCAL TOMATO DAY

It is not good that a nation which has the possibility of supplying all of its needs locally should devote itself solely to the production of one or two profitable items that can be exported everywhere for big-time bucks. What happens if lines of communication are cut off or tastes change? This was already a disastrous problem bringing about the mass migration of the Sea Peoples in ancient times. Modern African countries dedicated entirely to nut production and even that of oil have experienced similar difficulties. New Jersey once was "the Garden State." Now it is a highway. This is not healthy, and requires a toll to boot.

❡ End of the People's Crusade (1096)
❡ The Battle of Trafalgar (1805)

Thus Endeth SAVE THE NEIGHBORHOOD WEEK ∎

43 NOVUS ORDO SAECLORUM WEEK

Wherein is commemorated the entry of the one and only truly sanctifying grace into history. (1776 onwards)

10/22 CAN ANYTHING GOOD COME BEFORE 1776 DAY

Americanists believe that the appearance of their nation and its Magisterium is *the* significant event of all of history. How sad it makes them to think of those who lived before salvation was offered to the peoples of the world, and every valley was exalted and hill made low.

❡ Death of Charles Martel (741)
❡ The Three Emperors League (1873)
❡ Death of Cardinal Augustyn Hlond, Primate of Poland (1948)

10/23 MOS MAIORUM DAY

But where does Americanism come from? Partly, it is an inheritance from the Anglo-Saxons and their traditional dislike of doing things differently from what has been handed down to them: lest they rock the boat of business as usual and disturb the humdrum social order.

❡ Pope John XXII's *Licet iuxta doctrinam*, against Marsilius of Padua and John of Jandum (1327)
❡ Meeting of Hitler and Franco at Hendaye (1940)

III. CONSEQUENCE SEASON: OCTOBER   125

10/24 ROCK OF AGES DAY

Another element in the formation of Americanism is that coming from Puritanism, with its conviction of the need for a radical reformation of religious practice.
- The Treaty of Westphalia (1648)
- French Revolutionary Calendar (1793)
- Birth of the United Nations Organization (1945)

10/25 NOAH'S ARK DAY

The Puritans were convinced that they needed to get away from a wicked Old World to come to a New Jerusalem that could serve as a City on a Hill. Its City Charter would offer itself as a saintly model for the sinners trapped outside the Ark of Salvation.
- King Afonso I of Portugal occupies Lisbon (1147)
- Battle of Agincourt (1415)
- George III becomes King of Great Britain (1760)

10/26 ALL AND SUNDRY DAY

Americanism also grew out of the problem presented by peoples from a seemingly endless diversity of ethnic backgrounds and cultures pouring into the United States, especially from 1848 onwards.
- Death of Gilles de Rais (1440)
- Birth of Danton (1759)

10/27 KEEP 'EM OUT DAY

Many Americans, like the Nativists and Know-Nothings, deeply concerned for the purity of the Salvific Ark, wished to keep these fetid refugees from Old World corruption out of Eden.
- Birth of Count Raymond of Toulouse (1156)
- Death of Michael Servetus (1553)
- Chambord refuses the Tricolour (1873)
- Prayer Gathering in Assisi (1986)

10/28 REIN 'EM IN DAY

Other Americans believed that the way to keep the Salvific Ark of Noah pure was to make certain that the rest of the world shared its incontestable benefits...whether it wanted to or not. Invincible ignorance is no excuse for resisting the Way of Perfection.

¶ Birth of Bishop Cornelius Jansenius of Ypres (1585)
¶ Surrender of La Rochelle (1628)
¶ Death of John Locke (1704)
¶ Birth of Peter Paul Cahensly (1838)
¶ Statue of Liberty (1886)
¶ March on Rome (1922)

Thus Endeth NOVUS ORDO SAECLORUM WEEK ■

44 TUMULTUOUS MONOTONY WEEK

Wherein is commemorated the fact that The Ark of Salvation is actually headed nowhere. (1776 onwards)

10/29 I REMEMBER MAMA DAY

History did not begin in 1492 or 1776. All that happened at those dates was that representatives of old existing cultures found a new venue in which potentially to disfigure their old existing cultures.

¶ Closing of Port Royal (1709)
¶ Death of Jean d'Alembert (1783)
¶ Birth of Abraham Kuyper (1837), Founder of the Dutch Anti-Revolutionary Party
¶ Failure of the Emperor Charles' second attempt at a return to Hungary (1921)

10/30 DON'T ROCK THE BOAT DAY

The Anglo-Saxon tradition in America, which we have seen did not want to permit anyone or anything to "rock the humdrum social boat," found itself in an increasingly difficult situation given the number of diverse and potentially boat-rocking groups populating the country after 1848.

¶ Queen Isabella of Spain bans violence against Indians in America (1503)

¶ Birth of Ezra Pound (1885)

¶ Jesse James' gang robs bank in Lexington, Missouri (1866)

¶ October Manifesto of Nicholas II (1905)

¶ Humiliation of Cardinal Ottaviani at Second Vatican Council (1962)

10/31 SCHIZOPHRENIA DAY

A love of unthinking custom might be an Anglo-Saxon contribution to the Americanist Dogma, but its Puritan counterpart, with its emphasis on destruction of the communal past, worked to rock the immovable Bark of the New Jerusalem a great deal, religiously and politically. This passion increased in intensity and significance once secularized Puritans adapted their original individualist-rooted principles to a demand for personal freedom in all realms. Thus was created an Anglo-Saxon/Puritan-driven schizophrenia in which a passion for order and freedom was expressed by Americanists with an equal fervor.

¶ The Ninety-Five Theses (1517)

¶ Birth of Bishop Etienne Bernier of Orléans (1762)

¶ Carlist uprising in Spain (1900)

November

11/1 MULTIPLICATION DAY

The only way that it seemed that the existing order could be maintained in a land of diverse migrant groups dedicated simultaneously to a principle of anarchical freedom was by setting all such disruptive forces against one another, thereby multiplying factions to the utmost degree. This appeared to render utterly impossible a victory of any group that was seeking fulfillment of some significant boat-rocking goal that was contested by other potentially equally disruptive social forces. What was being stimulated was a permanent war of all against all, ever expanding in its extent, as the number of diverse, immigrant participants in the battle grew.

- ¶ Prague Manifesto of Müntzer (1521)
- ¶ Lisbon Earthquake (1755)
- ¶ *Immortale Dei* (1885)
- ¶ *Munificentissimus Deus* defining the Assumption (1950)

11/2 SUCKING DRY AND STICKING A FINGER IN YOUR NOSE DAY

It is dangerous for each group to use its freedom to promote distinct ideas and a distinct culture. It could be "divisive." Hence, each one has to learn to strip away its offensive distinctiveness and fit in with all the others. How mystical and mysterious were the ways of a liberty beyond compare in the history of the world! Sameness and diversity! Now and forever! One and inseparable!

III. CONSEQUENCE SEASON: NOVEMBER 129

❡ *Coelestis Pastor* vs. Molinos (1687)
❡ Birth of Marie Antoinette (1755)
❡ Nationalization of Church property in France (1789)
❡ French Directory established (1795)
❡ Sonderbund War (November 2–24, 1847)
❡ Death of George Bernard Shaw (1950)

11/3 SYSTEMATIC SIN DAY

The only permissible application of freedom for a given group or individual is really on the level of what can be instinctively understood by all other groups and individuals; i.e., their common animal instincts. Given the liberty to pursue these sole "integrating" goals, but not the historically "divisive" ones connected with a hunt for the True, the Good and the Beautiful preventing their abuse, "free men" are inexorably led down the pathway to a base and sinful existence. In other words, the *pluribus* become *unum* through the systematic encouragement of sin.

❡ First Act of Supremacy (1534)
❡ Birth of Marcellino Menéndez Pelayo (1856)
❡ Battle of Mentana (1867)

11/4 E PLURIBUS NOTHING DAY

Christianity protected diversity by insisting on self-abandonment to the Son of God, the imitation of whom corrects, perfects and brings into relief all of the personal distinctions of individuals; i.e., *ex unitate, plures*. Looking to one's boring, sinful self for guidance achieves nothing other than the confirmation of a drab, fallen uniformity. "*E pluribus — nihil; nada; rien de rien; nothing.*"

❡ Cardinal Wolsey arrested (1529)
❡ Cavour as Prime Minister (1852)

Thus Endeth TUMULTUOUS MONOTONY WEEK ■

45 LOBOTOMY WEEK

Wherein is commemorated the unbearable weight of a thick head oppressing the bulk of the body. (1900s)

11/5 INTEGRAL CONFUSION DAY

Jacques Maritain felt that all groups seeking goals using similar words and making reference to similar ideas shared some sort of analogical unity. Thus, Catholics and Communists, both claiming to pursue the attainment of "human dignity," were unified by commitment to the letters composing this phrase if nothing else.
- Council of Constance opens (1414)
- Gunpowder Plot (1605)
- Landing of William of Orange in England (1688)
- Foundation of the Catholic Truth Society (1884)

11/6 BECOMING A PERSON DAY

Personalism, as its name indicates, was concerned for the production of persons as opposed to individuals, who were said to be trapped in themselves and in their parochial world views.
- Philippe Egalité hoisted on his own petard (1793)
- October (November) Revolution in Russia (1917)

11/7 ONE MYSTIQUE LEADS TO ANOTHER DAY

Persons were said to be created by abandoning oneself as an individual to the mystique of a group with a particular energy that wished to affirm itself. There could be as many of these as there were particularly enthusiastic forces.
- Jean Baptiste Gobel denounces his priesthood and episcopacy (1793)

III. CONSEQUENCE SEASON: NOVEMBER

❡ Birth of Leon Trotsky—Lev Davidovitch Bronstein (1874)

❡ Birth of Bishop José de Jesus Manriquez y Zárate of Huejutla (1884)

11/8 BOOK BURNING DAY

Many Personalists believed that it was not possible to accept and promote the various energetic mystiques surrounding modern man unless a committed connection with one's own culture and the training designed to understand it were rejected.

❡ Battle of White Mountain (1620)
❡ Belgian Union (1828)
❡ Karl Freiherr von Vogelsang's death (1890)
❡ Abraham Kuyper's death (1920)

11/9 DOWN THE MEMORY HOLE DAY—ZANY DIVERSITY DAY

The result of this enterprise would be that whole cultures would disappear down the memory hole very quickly, only to be replaced by the "zany diversity" that an entertainment-driven civilization can produce. This hunt for entertaining diversity is itself guided by an elite that is stimulated by—exactly what?

❡ The Coup of 18 Brumaire (1799)
❡ *Qui pluribus* (1846)

11/10 LOST IN SPACE DAY

Is one fearful of precisely where the acceptance of many irrational mystiques would lead? There is no need to fear, Teilhard de Chardin assured us. The Holy Spirit was leading all natural mystiques, considered contradictory by those of little Faith, to a mysterious union under the Cosmic Christ through the leadership of the Holy Spirit.

⁋ The dream of René Descartes (1619)
⁋ Goddess of Reason (1793) in Notre Dame
⁋ Death of Fr. Diego Antonio Feijó (1843)
⁋ Stanley encounters Livingstone (1871)

11/11 THEY DIE AND YET THEY SMILE DAY

A slavish abandonment to all vigorous mystiques was indeed, in practice, ensuring the death of established cultures. Once again, the faithless had to be taught to abandon their disquiet and believe. The Holy Spirit was urging them to chuckle through their demise.

⁋ Fourth Lateran Council (11–30, 1215)
⁋ Election of Martin V (1417)
⁋ Mayflower Compact (1620)
⁋ Day of Dupes (1630)
⁋ Execution of Fra Diavolo (1806)
⁋ British begin Concentration Camps in South Africa (1900)

Thus Endeth LOBOTOMY WEEK ■

46 SAUVE QUI PEUT WEEK

Wherein are commemorated the efforts of the scattered remnants of Western Civilization to seek out perches from which to hang onto for dear life. (1900s)

11/12 THANKS, BUT NO THANKS DAY

The nineteenth and twentieth centuries have been filled with people who have rejected the spirit and much of the form of what modernity has to offer them.

⁋ John XXII *Cum inter nonnullus* on Franciscan poverty (1323)
⁋ Jacobins closed (1794)

III. CONSEQUENCE SEASON: NOVEMBER

℣ Toast of Archbishop Charles Cardinal Lavigerie of Algiers (1890)

℣ Emperor Charles of Austria-Hungary abdicates (12–13, 1918)

11/13 EVERYONE'S GONE TO THE MALL DAY

Some thought that the city centers were the problem and fled to the suburbs and countryside, only to discover that modernity was pursuing them there as well.

℣ Death of St. Nicholas I (867)

℣ *Iniunctum nobis* for Profession of Faith of Council of Trent (1565)

℣ Synod of Dort (1618)

℣ Opening of Catholic University (1889)

11/14 EVERY MOVE YOU MAKE DAY

A failure to understand the theological, philosophical, historical, sociological and psychological aspects of the modern world lead people who instinctively wish to escape it to adopt one form or another of its basic errors.

℣ Conquistadors arrive in Inca Empire (1533)

℣ Russian Civil War ends with Wrangel's flight (1920)

℣ Communist Party of Spain is created (1921)

℣ Stalin's victory over Trotsky and Zinoviev (1927)

11/15 BACK TO THE ROOTS DAY

The only way to grasp the full nature of modernity's mistake is by going back to the roots of our civilization to understand its character and what it is that distorted it so badly.

℣ Birth of Jacques Hébert (1757)

℣ End of *l'Avenir* (1831)

℣ Death of Pellegrino Rossi (1848)

11/16 DANGEROUS ISOLATION DAY

Alas! Discovery of the extent of the evil can lead one to a feeling of isolation that is dangerous for a person's psychological health.
- ¶ Death of Pierre Nicole (1695)
- ¶ Noyades of Nantes (1793)
- ¶ Birth of Léon Daudet (1867)
- ¶ Menshevik/Bolshevik split (1903)
- ¶ Death of Charles Maurras (1952)

11/17 HANGMAN'S HUMOR DAY

An absolutely essential way of dealing with the problem of modernity is to maintain one's sense of humor under whatever conditions of life he is living and to remember that it is the spirit of the corrupt civilization which is at fault—not its cities or countryside as such.
- ¶ Death of Pico della Mirandola (1494)
- ¶ Death of Reginald Pole (1558)
- ¶ Death of Queen Mary (1558)

11/18 THAT WHICH DOES NOT DESTROY ME MAKES ME STRONGER DAY

Friedrich Nietzsche is indeed part of the problem, but one of his aphorisms contains a truth pertinent to the situation of Traditionalists today: "that which does not destroy us makes us stronger."
- ¶ *Unam Sanctam* (1302)
- ¶ Birth of Jacques Maritain (1882)

Thus Endeth SAUVE QUI PEUT WEEK *and, with it,* CONSEQUENCE SEASON ■

IV. DENIAL SEASON

"Hey! I'm not the only one!"
(FROM ADAM & EVE TO THE PRESENT)

47 POINTING WEEK

Wherein are commemorated the efforts of those responsible for the modern nightmare to identify and expel the innocent from polite society. (1000s onwards)

11/19 IT'S THE POPE DAY

The lawyers, conciliarists and heretics of the later Middle Ages argued that society would function smoothly only if the Pope were put in his place. Things were falling apart because he was not being cut down to size.
- ¶ Pope Clement VII (1523)
- ¶ The Mayflower reaches Cape Cod (1620)

11/20 IT'S THE SCHOLASTICS DAY

The Renaissance, with its literary concerns, was convinced that things were falling apart because of the logical obsessions of scholastic thinkers. Get rid of them and all would be well. Little did it know that it was also promoting twentieth century New Theology.
- ¶ Attack on Jesuits in Naples (1767)
- ¶ Imprisonment of Droste-Vischering (1837)
- ¶ *Mediator Dei* (1947)

11/21 IT'S THE ANABAPTISTS DAY

Mainline Protestants admitted certain problems with the areas affected by their reforms. If only the "Enthusiasts"—the radicals, like the Anabaptists—were not on the scene to abuse the insights of a Luther or a Calvin!

¶ Birth of Friedrich Schleiermacher (1768)

¶ Birth of Archbishop Clemente de Jésus Munguía of Michoacán (1810)

¶ Death of Franz Josef (1916)

11/22 IT'S THE CHRISTIANS DAY

Naturalist Enlightenment thinkers argued that the problems of life would be dealt with if only the "infamous thing," the monstrous civilization deformed by Christianity, were abolished.

¶ Birth of Madame Sophie Swetchine (1782)

¶ Birth of André Gide (1869)

11/23 IT'S THE OTHER WING OF THE ENLIGHTENMENT DAY

Mechanists of the Enlightenment thought that inexorable scientific laws allowing no scope for individual freedom must rule the roost. Atomists, in contrast, argued that pure freedom should be the boss, with no space left for ironclad laws unnaturally imprisoning the individual and his will. Each blamed the other for wreaking havoc with life.

¶ Birth of Emperor Otto I (912)

¶ Death of Louis de Bonald (1840)

¶ Martyrdom of Fr. Miguel Pro (1927)

11/24 IT'S INTOLERANCE DAY

The Americanist pluralists were convinced that all ideas and all cultures could be mixed together. Problems only came from failure to allow tolerance for all of these—and

the reduction of their practical effect to nothing other than meaningless production and consumption.
- ¶ End of the Siege of Zara (1202)
- ¶ Birth of Spinoza (1632)
- ¶ Death of Fr. Lorenzo Ricci, S.J. (1775)
- ¶ Adoption of Revolutionary Calendar (1793)
- ¶ Birth of Fr. Luigi Taparelli d'Azeglio, S.J. (1793)
- ¶ Pope flees to Gaeta (1848)
- ¶ Death of Georges Clemenceau (1929)

11/25 IT'S EVERYTHING WE BELIEVED UNTIL YESTERDAY DAY

Conservatives of all stripes are firm defenders of whatever exists. If what exists today does not exist tomorrow, then what exists today must be abandoned with the same fervor that it was defended yesterday.
- ¶ Paris condemns Ockham's books (1339)
- ¶ Birth of General Augusto Pinochet (1915)

Thus Endeth POINTING WEEK ■

48 J'ACCUSE WEEK

Wherein is commemorated the erection of a more accurate target for sharpshooting pleasure. (1200s onwards)

11/26 THOMAS MORE DAY

The Legalists, from the time of Philip the Fair onwards, were building a world where only power counted. Hence, the willingness to blatantly play with Truth and Justice, always disguising what one was doing with reference to the need for "public order."
- ¶ Jesuits expelled from France (1764)
- ¶ Death of Adam Mickiewiecz (1855)
- ¶ Birth of Don Luigi Sturzo (1871)

11/27 ANTI-GORGIAS AND PROTAGORAS DAY

The Renaissance, and then the Enlightenment, wanted to displace Aristotelian logic. Alas, those who live by Sophism, die by Sophism.

¶ Council of Clermont (1095)
¶ Oath to Civil Constitution imposed (1790)
¶ Miraculous Medal (1830)
¶ Birth of Bishop Vital Maria Gonçalves de Oliveira (1844)

11/28 BOSSUET DAY

Protestant principles end by justifying irrational, personal, charismatic manipulation of texts and truths. They also lead to the potential for endless division, as was already clear by the 1600s.

¶ *Super soliditate* vs. Febronianism (1786)
¶ Birth of Friedrich Engels (1820)

11/29 DIALOGUE OF THE CARMELITES DAY

The attack on the supernatural realm as a dangerous obstacle to natural development created the image of believers as parasitic sub-human sores on the body politic. Hence, Modernity developed its willingness to brutally dispense with such useless trash. Unfortunately, each more powerful faction added its less powerful, but still pro-revolutionary competitors to the list of parasites.

¶ Death of Philip the Fair (1314)
¶ Death of Fr. Michael of Cesena (1342)
¶ Death of Edmond Richer (1631)
¶ Punctation of Olmütz (1850)
¶ Birth of C.S. Lewis (1898)

11/30 SYLLABUS OF ERRORS DAY

The whole of modernity was shot through with erroneous, self-destructive principles. Identifying them was the goal of Pope Pius IX's *Syllabus of Errors* (1864).

¶ *Laetare Jerusalem* (1544)

¶ Codreanu garrotted (1938)

December

12/1 MOAT AND FENCE DAY

One ought to be intolerant of things that are untruthful and unjust, lest they win out and destroy the good while claiming that they are being tolerant of it. Moats and fences serve their purpose in a difficult world. There are no friends without enemies.

- ¶ Martyrdom of Fr. Edmund Campion, S.J. (1581)
- ¶ Birth of Fr. Gustave François Xavier de Ravignan, S.J. (1795)
- ¶ Plutarco Elías Calles, President of Mexico (1924)
- ¶ Sergei Kirov Assassination (1934)

12/2 OPEN YOUR EYES DAY

Shutting one's eyes to the truth or falsity of a given energetic group was not a guarantee that the Holy Spirit would guide the enthusiast to safe port. It was a recipe for fanaticism.

- ¶ Napoleon becomes the Emperor (1804)
- ¶ Battle of Austerlitz (1805)
- ¶ Death of Fr. Vincent de Paul Bailly (1912)
- ¶ Franz Josef becomes Emperor of Austria (1848)
- ¶ Coup d'état of Prince President Louis-Napoleon (1851)

Thus Endeth J'ACCUSE WEEK ■

49 POSEUR WEEK

Wherein is commemorated the justification of some vices by the cultivation of other vices. (1900s to the present)

12/3 JUTTING CHIN DAY

Those who are at the forefront of modernity have to cover their flaws by looking intelligent, soulful, authoritative and compassionate at one and the same time. The right pipe helps; so does the right hat. Even better is the correct thrust forward of the chin.

¶ First Covenant of Protestant Scots (1557)
¶ Death of Mary Baker Eddy (1910)

12/4 BAUHAUS DAY

Artistic madness can be covered by a great deal of sneering at the stupidity of those who fail to understand one's own obvious genius. It is important to remember to demand humor from everyone else, chastising lack of it as a sign of totalitarian aspirations, while possessing none oneself, since there are some matters that are "too serious" for joking.

¶ Judging of Pope John XII (963)
¶ End of the Council of Trent (1563)
¶ Death of Cardinal Richelieu (1642)
¶ Birth of Francisco Franco (1892)
¶ Death of the Marquis François-René de la Tour du Pin (1924)

12/5 LAMENTING ONE'S PERVERSITY DAY

Of course, some people recognize that they are guilty of various flaws. To err is human! To forgive, divine! After having divinely forgiven themselves, the Modernists change nothing and proceed along their same, unchanging path to perdition.

¶ Death of Mozart (1791)
¶ Soviet Constitution (1936)

12/6 SEE HOW MUCH I WORK DAY

Modern man prides himself on his work. Therefore, he competes with others to demonstrate just how little time he has left over from his important enterprises. How he can perform his tasks seriously if he has so little chance to breathe is another question.

¶ Birth of Archbishop Victor Auguste Cardinal Dechamps of Mâlines (1810)
¶ Catholic-Calvinist alliance in the Netherlands (1888)
¶ Abrogation of the Concordat (1905)

12/7 SEE HOW SENSITIVE I AM DAY

But the working hero of modernity also has to insist, at least vocally, upon his compassion. And compassionate he is, so long as that towards which he is being sensitive is another of his naturalist flaws.

¶ Declaration of the Holy Office against the Jansenists (1690)
¶ Birth of Gabriel Marcel (1889)
¶ Foundation of the *Cattolica* in Milan (1921)

12/8 COCKTAIL PARTY EDUCATION DAY

Intelligence is essential to the working, compassionate man. Alas! He has almost no time to obtain it. Still, bits and pieces of impressive phrases can be strung together to make conversation with other equally pressed individuals at cocktail parties.

¶ *Ineffabilis Deus*: Apostolic Constitution on Dogma of the Immaculate Conception (1854)

IV. DENIAL SEASON: DECEMBER   143

⁋ *Syllabus of Errors* (1864)
⁋ Death of Herbert Spencer (1903)
⁋ Death of John Lennon (1980)

12/9 DANGERLESS OUTRAGE DAY

Modern man is also fearless. He says so often enough. But that fearlessness cannot interfere with work or with pleasure. It is best to be fearless about past historical events. Fearlessness in dangerous contemporary circumstances can prove to be just that: dangerous.

⁋ Our Lady of Guadalupe apparition (1531)
⁋ *Singulari quadam*: Pius IX's Allocution on Dogma of Immaculate Conception (1854)
⁋ Anarchist bomb in Chamber of Deputies (1893)
⁋ Denunciation of the French Concordat (1905)

Thus Endeth POSEUR WEEK ■

50 AUTHENTICITY WEEK

Wherein is commemorated the moment for that consistency which is the "hobgoblin of little minds" to have its place in the sun. (1900s onwards)

12/10 ALL YE HUMBLY VIRILE DAY

Virility does not have to be proclaimed to exist. In fact, its proclamation already makes it a suspicious phenomenon. It gains by humility.

⁋ Michael Paphlagon, Byzantium Emperor dies of results of dropsy (1041)
⁋ Martin Luther burns papal edict (1520)
⁋ Trial of King Louis XVI opens (1792)
⁋ Pulpit Law (1871)

12/11 ALL YE STARVING ARTISTS DAY

There is not much room left in the modern world for those creative people who do not toe the party line of the style that is in season—and for that season only—to survive.

¶ Sonderbund established (1845)
¶ *Gravissimas inter* vs. Jakob Frohschammer (1862)
¶ Birth of Solzhenitsyn (1918)
¶ *Quas primas* and the Feast of Christ the King (1925)

12/12 ALL YE PAINFULLY EMBARRASSED DAY

Sins, when recognized, need to be rejected. There are sinners who recognize what they have done. The usual response is a painful embarrassment—and repentance.

¶ Vendée defeat at Le Mans (1793)
¶ Papal nuncio expelled from Switzerland (1873)
¶ Anticlerical forces oppose the Fourth Centenary of Our Lady of Guadalupe (1931)

12/13 ALL YE HOPELESSLY EXHAUSTED DAY

Sensible human beings realize that work is draining, and that the modern world so drains one that nothing other than mindless behavior can generally follow a day bent under its demands.

¶ Death of Frederick II (1250)
¶ Abdication of Celestine V (1294)
¶ Opening of the Council of Trent (1545)
¶ Foundation of the Catholic Center Party (1870)

12/14 ALL YE STRUGGLING FRIENDS AND COUPLES DAY

It is extremely difficult for friends and couples to maintain their loyalty and their moral obligations in a world where all of the institutions, the economy

IV. DENIAL SEASON: DECEMBER   145

and the entertainment system urge them to do the exact opposite.

¶ Mitraillades in Lyon (1793)

¶ Death of George Washington (1799)

¶ Assassination of Sidonio Pais, democratic dictator of Portugal (1918)

12/15 ALL YE UNPUBLISHED SCHOLARS DAY

How much work is left in the shadows or not even undertaken because of the domination of the publishing world either by enemies of the truth or friends purely of the profit motive?

¶ Assassination of Pope John VIII (882)

¶ All French occupied lands ordered to adopt revolutionary institutions (1792)

¶ Birth of Bishop Bernard John McQuaid of Rochester (1823)

12/16 ALL YE EXPOSED NECKS DAY

The anti-modernists are the ones who really risk their careers and their lives in the current environment. They suffer the penalty not only of being destroyed, physically, but also of being identified as cruel oppressors even as they themselves are brutally crushed.

¶ Birth of François Quesnay, leader of the Physiocrats (1694)

¶ Death of Rasputin, Old Calendar (1916)

¶ Confederation of Autonomous Right Wing Groups gains in Spain (1934)

Thus Endeth AUTHENTICITY WEEK ∎

51 IF NOT US, IT'S THE FASCISTS WEEK: THEIR VERSION

Wherein is commemorated a certain rediscovery of sin, which, happily, is found to have no hold over powerful oligarchies. (1945 onwards)

12/17 BECAUSE OUR NAME IS DIFFERENT DAY

Fascists are people who bear the name Fascist. We do not call ourselves Fascists. We fought Fascists. Therefore, only our enemies can be Fascists.

¶ King Totila conquers Rome (546)
¶ Amiens receives the skull of St. John the Baptist (1206)
¶ Anti-Saloon League of America, Washington, D.C. (1895)
¶ 1st prize of 100,000 francs offered for communications with Extraterrestrials (1900)
¶ First Airplane Flight (1903)

12/18 BECAUSE WE'RE POWERFUL DAY

The United States and the Soviet Union won the war against the Fascists. They were strong and they said that they were not Fascists. Therefore, you were hit on the head if you did not say that it was their enemies who were Fascists and that they could not possibly be Fascist in character.

¶ Battle of Verdun ends (1916)
¶ Prohibition is passed by the US Congress and sent to the states (1917)
¶ Foundation of Le Monde (1944)

IV. DENIAL SEASON: DECEMBER

12/19 BECAUSE WE GOT A JUMP ON THE OTHERS DAY

It became ridiculous to call many differing people Fascists. Whoever used the terminology after the War first had the edge on others trying to adopt it. The United States and the Soviet Union were first. Therefore, their enemies were indeed Fascists.

¶ Thomas Paine's first "American Crisis" essay (1776)
¶ Royalists lose Toulon (1793)
¶ Dicken's anti-Utilitarian "A Christmas Carol" published (1843)

12/20 BECAUSE WE'VE ABOLISHED HISTORY DAY

Why would you want to learn, historically and philosophically, exactly what Fascism is? Fascism is what we have told you that it is. Anyone delving deeper into its study must himself be a Fascist! Censorship against those seeking to find out what Fascism really is cannot be censorship. Saying it is censorship is censorship.

¶ John Hughes, Bishop of New York (1842)
¶ Pius X's Decree on Frequent Communion (1905)

12/21 BECAUSE ONLY SOMEONE ON THE RUBBISH HEAP OF HISTORY WOULD THINK OTHERWISE DAY

Of course, there were people who did not seem to be Fascists themselves who persisted in accusing the victors of Fascist behavior. Why would they do so? From the Soviet standpoint, it was because of the absurd Fascist class outlook of the Fascist idiot engaged in Fascist lies.

¶ Birth of Jean-Henri Fabre (1823)
¶ Birth of Prince Pyotr Kropotkin (1842)
¶ *Tuas libenter* on the Congress of Munich (1863)

12/22 BECAUSE ONLY A RED WOULD THINK OTHERWISE DAY

From the Pluralist standpoint, the person accusing the "Free World" of Fascist tendencies, if not a Fascist himself, must be part of what rapidly, after the War, became fair game for being accused of Fascism along with the real thing: the Red World Fascists.

- ¶ Capture of Rhodes (1522)
- ¶ Birth of Fr. Clemens Schrader, S.J. (1820)
- ¶ Death of Isaac Hecker (1888)
- ¶ Dreyfus convicted (1894)

12/23 BECAUSE ONLY A MADMAN WOULD THINK OTHERWISE DAY

Still, why bring politics into the picture, disturbing the united front of the old war days? Someone accusing either the Soviets or the Pluralists of Fascism was clearly a madman! Bring out the drugs! Bring in the psychiatrists! Tie the Fascist lunatic to his bed!

- ¶ *Ex supremae clementiae dono* vs. Dionysius Foullechat (1368)
- ¶ Murder of the Duc de Guise (1588)
- ¶ *Magnus Dominus*-Bull of Union (1595)
- ¶ James II escapes (1688)
- ¶ Defeat of the Vendée heroes at the Battle of Savenay (1793)
- ¶ Birth of St. Antonio Maria Claret (1807)
- ¶ *Ubi arcano*—On the Peace of Christ in the Reign of Christ (1922)
- ¶ Testament of Lenin (1922)

Thus Endeth THEIR VERSION OF IF NOT US, IT'S THE FASCISTS WEEK ■

IV. DENIAL SEASON: DECEMBER   149

52 IF NOT US, IT'S THE FASCISTS WEEK: OUR VERSION

Wherein is commemorated the calling of a spade a spade. (1945 onwards)

12/24 YOU RIDE THE TRAIN, YOU PAY THE FARE DAY

One really cannot flee the Socratic principle of non-contradiction. Something cannot be true and false at the same time. You got what you deserved. Accept it like a man.

¶ First Holy Year since 1775 proclaimed (1825)

¶ Birth of "Saint" Anthony Fauci—Covid Messiah (1940)

12/25 WHAT'S LEFT BUT IRRATIONAL FAITH DAY

In fact, insofar as one truly, in his heart of hearts, insists that his ideas did not have the consequences that they obviously do have, it demonstrates that his *modus operandi* is really that of a Faith, and—qualitatively different from the Catholic Faith—an irrational one, that does not see why logic should apply to it at all.

¶ Charlemagne Crowned as Emperor (800)

¶ Stephen crowned King of Hungary—some sources say January 1, 1001 (1000)

¶ Games prohibited in Plymouth (1625)

¶ Birth of José Manuel Groot, Catholic polemicist (1800)

¶ Foundation of the Assumptionists by Emmanuel d'Alzon (1845)

¶ Conversion of Paul Claudel (1886)

¶ Death of Peter Paul Cahensly of St. Raphael Verein; hated by Americanists (1923)

12/26 WHAT'S LEFT BUT WILLFULNESS DAY

Insofar as one insists that he does not wish his ideas to have these consequences, the analogy with Fascism becomes still more clear. The Triumph of the Will remains the guiding principle.

¶ Death of Claude-Adrien Helvetius (1771)
¶ Birth of Mao (1893)
¶ Arrest of Cardinal Mindszenty (1948)

12/27 WHAT'S LEFT BUT BRUTE FORCE DAY

In fact, with Reason exiled from the picture, the only way that the contradictory will of confused modern man can ever be maintained is by the application of brute force. At least, that is to say, until nature itself revolts against its own violation.

¶ Birth of St. Joseph Pignatelli (1737)
¶ Assassination of General Léonard Duphot in Rome (1797)

12/28 ILLOGICAL REMNANT DAY

Until the day of nature's complete rejection of the irrationality and brutal willfulness of the contradictory ideology imposed upon it, it can only continue to survive due to the illogical retention, occasioned by a mindless conservatism, of some logical remnants of Truth that have not yet succumbed to the impact of the general madness.

¶ Death of Pierre Bayle (1706)
¶ End of the revolutionary cult of the *Decadi* (1800)
¶ *Quod apostolici muneris* on socialism (1878)

12/29 PRO-CHOICE DAY

Abortion is, perhaps, the most blatant crime of modernity, since it strikes at the most innocent. This, too, is a Fascist action, both historically as well as in its justification. Why not call its supporters the Pro-Triumph of the Will Party?

❡ Death of Becket (1170)

❡ Birth of Albert Pike, Freemason and possible Satanist (1809)

❡ Alfonso XII becomes King of Spain (1874)

❡ Prohibition of Action Française (1926)

12/30 CYNICAL COVER-UP DAY

Of course some of the supporters of modern barbarism know exactly what it is that they are doing. But why admit this openly? To paraphrase Cavour in speaking of Constitutions and Parliaments, it is possible to accomplish so much more by praising sweet-sounding words and seeming to be beholden to them!

❡ Arrival of Lamennais in Rome (1831)

❡ Murder of Rasputin (1916)

❡ Foundation of the Soviet Union (1922)

Thus Endeth OUR VERSION OF IF NOT US, IT'S THE FASCISTS WEEK *and, with it,* DENIAL SEASON ■

ADDENDA

12/31 FEAST OF ALL THE CATHOLICOPHOBES

Love means never having to say that you are sorry—for studied ignorance, vile slander, and barbaric cruelty. Come on! Let's accept the creeps for one day, and love them just the way they are!

❡ Vandal/Sueve/Alan invasion across the Rhine (406)

❡ Death of Wycliffe (1384)

❡ The last day of the French Revolutionary Calendar (1805)

¶ Birth of Fr. Léonce de Grandmaison, S.J. (1868)
¶ *Divini illius magistri* (1929)
¶ *Casti connubii* (1930)

2/29 YOU NEVER KNOW DAY

History throws curve balls. Although it may well seem that the Catholic worldview is completely dead, it could re-emerge stronger than ever. Think of the sociologist who would have finished his book on the character of Arabia the day before Mohammed began to preach in the city of Mecca.

¶ First people accused of witchcraft in Salem (1692)
¶ Marquis de Sade transferred from Vincennes to the Bastille (1784)

v.

Suggestions for Monthly Outbursts of Spontaneous Global Joy
(THE END OF HISTORY AND THE BEATIFIC VISION OF ETERNAL MODERNITY)

These monthly festivities, to be prepared with the fervent assistance of all Homeland Security forces, are intended for the properly ecstatic commemoration of the chief steps in the liberation of all of Genderkind from the insufferable chains forged in the darkest past by the principle of non-contradiction and the demands of mental health. Police must apprehend all unvaccinated Traditionalists who will most certainly look upon the festivities in a perverse spirit—apprehend and then deal with them accordingly.

January Protestant Liberation of the Individual from the Tyranny of Reason and Free Will

February Protestant Liberation of the Individual from the Mystical Body of Christ, All Rational Understanding of the Value of Natural Societies, and from the Under-Utilization of Willful State, Oligarchic and Charismatic Power

March Mechanist Naturalism's Liberation of Creation from Limits on "What Works"

April Atomistic Naturalism's Liberation of Creation from All Meaning and Purpose

May "Human Dignity's" Liberation from Any Possible Definition of "Human Dignity"

June The Willful Naturalist State's Liberation from Absolutely Everything Except Willful Oligarchies and Charismatic Powers

July Oligarchic and Charismatic Liberation from Absolutely Everything, Including Nature

August The Medical Profession's Liberation From Nature, Science and Curing Illnesses

September The Liberation of All Organs of Education and Information from the Pursuit of Truth, Goodness and Beauty—Except as Defined by the Authors of the Great Reset

October The Liberation of the Great Reset Magisterium from Everything Except the Will of Klaus Schwab, Bill Gates, George Soros & Company

November The Liberation of Klaus Schwab, Bill Gates, George Soros & Company from Everything other than Eugenics and Satanism

December The Church's Liberation from Any Other Mission than Adulating All These Other Liberations More Speedily and More Slavishly Than Every Other Institution in the The Long History of the World's Craven Groveling Before the Forces of Evil

ABOUT THE AUTHOR

JOHN C. RAO obtained his doctorate in Modern European History from Oxford University in 1977. He worked in 1978–1979 as Eastern Director of the Intercollegiate Studies Institute in Bryn Mawr, PA, and was Associate Professor of European History at St. John's University in New York City from 1979 to 2021. Dr. Rao is also director of the Roman Forum, a Catholic cultural organization founded by the late Professor Dietrich von Hildebrand in 1968. He writes for numerous French, German, Spanish and Italian journals. Perhaps the most important of his works are *Americanism and the Collapse of the Church in the United States* (Roman Forum Press, 1995), *Black Legends and the Light of the World* (Remnant Press, 2012), *Removing the Blindfold* (Angelus Press, 2014), a discussion of Catholics rediscovering their own heritage in the post-French revolutionary era, and *A Centenary Meditation on a Quest for "Purification" Gone Mad* (Arouca Press, 2019).

www.ingramcontent.com/pod-product-compliance
Lightning Source LLC
Chambersburg PA
CBHW021426070526
44577CB00001B/76